The

RAVEN & I

CONFESSIONS OF A WOODEN BOAT LOVER

K. GORDON GREEN

Published by

 GENERAL STORE
GSPH PUBLISHING HOUSE

Box 28, 1694 Burnstown Road,
Burnstown, Ontario, Canada K0J 1G0
Telephone (613) 432-7697 or 1-800-465-6072

ISBN 1-894263-11-1
Printed and bound in Canada

Copyright 1999

Layout and Design by Derek McEwen
Illustrations by Paul Burke
Cover photograph by Tad Palmer
General Store Publishing House
Burnstown, Ontario, Canada

Canadian Cataloguing in Publication Data

Green, K. Gordon, 1934-
    The Raven and I : confessions of a wooden boat lover

ISBN 1-894263-11-1

    1. Boats and boating–Anecdotes.   2. Boats and boating–Humour.
I. Title.

GV777.3.G74 1999   797.1'02'07   C99-900759-9

CONTENTS

ACKNOWLEDGEMENTS

The characters in this book are real—only a few names have been changed. I thank all of these people for allowing me to share with others a piece of their past. I'm particularly grateful to Libby Frise and Heather and Gillian for their good-natured encouragement as I wrestled with the larger-than-life character of their late husband/father, John Frise, and to Bill McDonald for his help in re-creating long-forgotten incidents in John's life. Last but not least, a huge thank-you to John Stevens, without whose insight and support this book simply would not have happened.

FOR DI,

my soulmate through the years, who didn't complain too much when the Raven turned my head.

AREAS OF DETAIL

GEORGIAN BAY

LAKE HURON

L. MICHIGAN

L. HURON

L. ONTARIO

L. ERIE

Parry Sound

Go-Home Bay

Honey Harbour

Port Severn

Christian I.

Toanche

Penetanguishene

L. Couchiching

Orillia

Owen Sound

Barrie

L. SIMCOE

Toronto

45°

44°

81°

80°

0   50   Miles
0   50   Kilometers

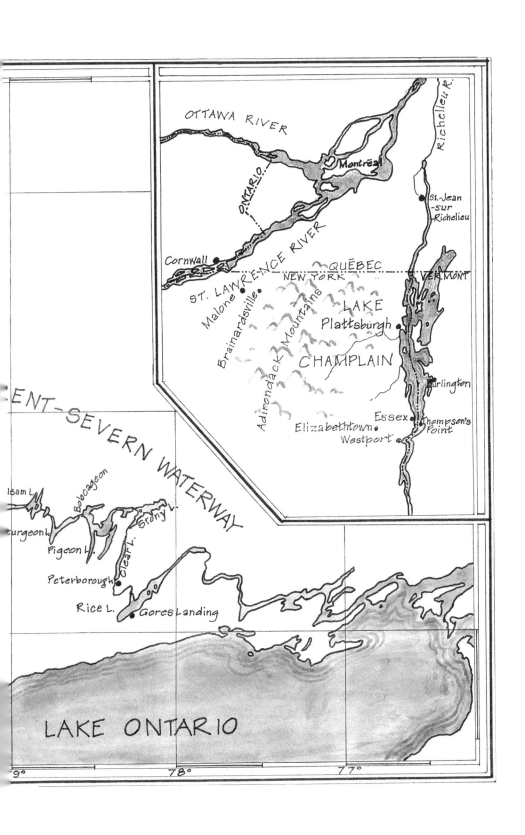

OTTAWA RIVER

Montréal

Richelieu R.

St.-Jean
-sur
-Richelieu

ONTARIO

ST. LAWRENCE RIVER

Cornwall

QUÉBEC

NEW YORK VERMONT

Malone

Brainardsville

Adirondack Mountains

LAKE

Plattsburgh

CHAMPLAIN

Burlington

Essex
Thompson's
Point

Elizabethtown

Westport

ENT-SEVERN WATERWAY

Bobcaygeon

Isam L.

Sturgeon L.

Stony L.

Pigeon L.

Clear L.

Peterborough

Rice L.

Gores Landing

LAKE ONTARIO

79°   78°   77°

1

A Singular Character

I COULD JUST make out the white puff.

It was noon on a cloudless day in June 1972. From my office high in the Toronto-Dominion Centre in downtown Toronto I looked out over Lake Ontario shimmering under an improbably blue sky. I was tilted back with my feet on the air vent and my shoulder cradling the phone, trying to concentrate on what the lawyer was saying and wishing I was out there, not here.

The air was so clear I could see every detail of the New York shore. I squinted at the thin jagged line of the horizon, followed it to the point where New York becomes Ontario. Hanging above the border notch of the Niagara Gorge nearly 40 miles away was a tiny puff, the mist from the falls. The lawyer droned on.

Suddenly the door behind me burst open and a familiar voice filled the little space.

"Gordy, Baby, I've found her! I've found her at last!"

Wincing, I covered the phone and swivelled round. John Frise stood grinning in the open doorway, arms spread wide and newspaper in hand. He threw down the paper with a flourish – the classified section of Saturday's *Globe and Mail*.

I apologized to the lawyer and hung up, focussing on the ad circled in red:

RARE BEAUTY
22' 1958 Century Raven. Open cuddy day cruisr, all mahog, 160 H.P. V8, very fast, orig. owner, low hours. $1,800 firm. (705) 555-5678

"It's perfection," Frise looked at me triumphantly. "Exactly what I've been looking for."

"How d'you know?"

"Well, to start with I've seen her." A distant look came into his eyes as he shifted back to the feminine gender. "I drove out to Rice Lake yesterday. She's been owned by a doctor there who says he can't handle her any more – just pulled her out of the water two years ago and she's been pining in the shed ever since, poor thing."

"Why can't he handle her any more?"

"Gordy, you have to see her. She's a classic. Solid African mahogany stem to stern. Hull painted flat black. Big and beamy, and powerful. And her shape, for God's sakes. She's built like a Second World War battleship. Her sides go straight down into the water, straight down, I tell you. No camber at all. What grace!"

I didn't associate the word grace with what he had just described – it sounded more like a Centurion tank to me. But now John was going on and on, and was clearly smitten. He had been bursting into my office a lot like this ever since he'd begun his search for a large dependable boat. Each time a candidate was found he would go into raptures about its seaworthiness, solid construction and workmanlike lines. Now as he babbled on he was using emotive words like "classic," "graceful" and "sexy." This made me uneasy, though I couldn't explain why.

Frise's search for a replacement for his 18-foot lapstrake cedar Grew inboard had been going on for months. He felt he needed something more substantial to make the regular run to and from his summer cottage at Go-Home Bay, a place only accessible by water. Fierce westerlies frequently lashed that part of Georgian Bay, and part of the route from Honey Harbour to Go-Home was fully exposed to the open water. Perhaps he was envious of my venerable 24-foot double-planked mahogany Hunter; I certainly wasn't about to admit to him that this 1944 relic was a sponge held together by molasses.

"Have you already committed to buy her?"

"Course I have. Wrote a cheque on the spot. Eighteen hundred bucks is a steal."

"Hull okay?"

"Uh, well. She's been out of the water couple years so she's a bit dirty. Also the windshield somehow got smashed, and she needs a new top. But the guys at the marina are great. They're gonna fix her up right away. New windshield from the Century Boat Works in Manistee, Michigan. Fresh paint and varnish, the works. She'll be ready end next week."

"But what about the hull?"

"What d'you mean?" He looked at me blankly.

"John."

⤳ ⤳ ⤳

John Frise (as in "wise") was the youngest child and only son of Jimmy Frise, beloved *Toronto Star Weekly* cartoonist who teamed with humorist Greg Clarke in the 1930s and 1940s to provide a widely-read column of hilarity and human interest. An engineering graduate from University of Toronto who had spent his entire career in the investment business, John was anything but your run-of-the-mill investment banker. Outrageous was not too strong a word to describe him. You either loved his take on life or you found him boorish. From time to time I admittedly fell in the latter camp, but most often I was one of his biggest fans.

Truth is, John was fun to be with and often outlandishly funny, a character of extremes who had a heart wide as a country mile beneath his gruff and sarcastic exterior. When I joined Nesbitt Thomson in 1968 fresh out of business school, John was already a seasoned and successful member of the institutional equity department and he didn't let me forget it. It was a while before I even got to know him, for I was beneath his dignity, an over-educated stuffed shirt, a corporate finance type who had little practical knowledge of the financial markets. It was only when he discovered that we both owned cottages on Lake Huron's Georgian Bay and had wooden boats that he recognized a kindred spirit.

John loved being the centre of attention. I was soon to learn that, among other things, he was a confirmed hypochondriac, a condition that had its hilarious side even though it had some justification as he suffered from deteriorating health. He seemed unable to resist sharing his infirmities with any who would listen, particularly doctors. He revered doctors. Often at social functions he could be seen baring his anatomy before an astonished audience, particularly if there was a doctor present, to reveal the scars from his latest operation.

I remember visiting Frise in hospital after his back operation. I was accompanied by Bill Rogan, a Nesbitt colleague, and on entering the room we were confronted by this Oriental potentate-like figure propped against a mountain of pillows, surrounded by books, magazines and paraphernalia for the bedridden including a trapeze suspended from the ceiling and a recently-used glass bedbottle. John's face brightened when he saw us before resuming the tragic mien of the mortally afflicted. Rogan, still wearing his raincoat, thought to cheer our friend by flashing a concealed bottle of Glenfiddich. Growling his delight, Frise made a sweeping gesture with his right arm, delivering a coup de grâce to the bedbottle which was launched in a graceful arc, disgorging its golden contents over books, magazines and pillows before smashing loudly against the wall. A nurse came running in. "Oh nurse," said Frise not missing a beat, "my friends here have carelessly dropped my little bottle. Be a dear and clean it up?"

Tall and portly with generous jowls, prematurely silver hair and a face in perpetual motion, Frise was a born raconteur. His consuming passion was to live some experience so that he could later recount it to others with appropriate embellishments. He could hold forth on almost any subject and had opinions on most. As soon as he had built up a head of steam he was unstoppable. His voice would rise progressively as his hands carved the air in vigorous punctuation, easing his cuffs or adjusting his tie. When he reached the peak of his delivery he would suddenly stop and glance over his shoulder to make sure no aliens were listening. Then he would bring his face close to yours and conclude in an urgent whisper, easing back and looking at you piercingly, inhaling through taut lips. Often at this stage his tongue would make a brief appearance in final emphasis.

People who didn't know John well would often ask how I could have put up for so long with such an opinionated and bombastic individual.

The answer lay in the fact that, as John pursued his passion for intrigue and storytelling, he precipitated incidents as if by spontaneous combustion. The pleasure I derived from being a bit player in this process far outweighed any distress I felt from the occasional ruffled feather. And I wasn't alone. Over the years John attracted a whole coterie of friends, humble and famous, each in his or her own way similarly attracted to the aura surrounding this extraordinary Pied Piper.

During the early years of our acquaintance one of John's friends, a Toronto lawyer, was retained to represent Xaviera Hollander (the "Happy Hooker") on a Canadian tax matter. To John this represented a serious challenge: it became his sacred duty to meet this First Lady of the Night. So he undertook a campaign of intense wheedling and cajoling until his friend relented and arranged a clandestine rendezvous in the cocktail lounge of the former Four Seasons Motel on Jarvis Street.

John waited nervously with his friend, sitting at a small brass cocktail table in the darkest corner of the lounge. After a while he ordered a martini, then another. Finally the lady appeared, all modesty and smiles and full of apologies for being late. John was completely swept away. He leapt to his feet, stuck out his hand and blurted out "Hiya, Happy!" In the process he knocked over the table and sent his drink cascading down the front of Xaviera's dress.

History does not record the lady's response.

Xaviera was not the only famous person to come within John's sphere of influence. A legendary incident concerns Jack Nicklaus and the TDF golf clubs. John was house guest of one of his golfing buddies at Lost Tree, an exclusive gated community just north of West Palm Beach, Florida. He was relaxing after a late afternoon game of golf with several friends including Gordon Gray, the prominent Toronto realtor. Gray had developed the nearby Loxahatchee Club, which embraces a fine Jack Nicklaus designed golf course. He and Frise were both inveterate raconteurs, and soon they were swapping stories thick and fast, each topping the last, blissfully unaware of the prejudices of their day. Finally John reached deep into his reservoir and brought out one of his very best, the story of the Indian lad curious about how he got his name:

"Father, in what manner is it that our names are chosen?" asked the Brave with great respect, anxious not to betray the slightest dissatisfaction with his own name.

"Ah, my son, you who are already so wise in the ways of nature should know that in the ancient tradition of our forefathers a newborn must be named after the first thing encountered after birth. Thus your mother was named Stag-Drinking-By-The-Water after she beheld a deer with great antlers standing by the side of the lake as she was being carried from the birth tepee.

"In such a fashion too was your sister called Moon-Over-The-Pine-Tree, and I, Howling Wolf. But why do you ask, Two-Dogs-Fucking?"

John told the story masterfully, stringing out the dialogue with such deliberate, slow dignity that when he came to the punch line Gray, helpless with laughter, knew he was beaten and threw in the towel. But he kept the story, polishing it like a jewel, waiting for his opportunity. It came a few days later when he was dining at Loxahatchee with the great golfer Jack Nicklaus, a neighbour and raconteur in his own right. Giving credit to his friend John Frise, Gray delivered the story in the slow, grave cadences of a Chief Dan George. The results were explosive. By all accounts The Golden Bear was so weak-kneed that he had to be half-carried home. A few weeks later a new set of golf clubs arrived at Gray's house in Toronto, each clubhead engraved "TDF." Frise would later recount this tale with a mixture of pride and envy, for he always felt a strong proprietary interest in those TDF golf clubs.

ॐ ॐ ॐ

After his most recent visit to my office, John phoned the marina long distance each morning to check on the boat's progress, to be assured with progressive testiness that all was on schedule. Toward the end of the second week he called me and suggested lunch at his club to discuss how he would take delivery of his new pride and joy. A whiff of spontaneous combustion was in the air.

2

The Raven Awakes

THE NATIONAL CLUB imposes its brass-plaqued presence on Bay Street just north of King Street in the heart of Toronto's financial district. In 1971 it was exclusively a male domain, a luncheon and dining club comfortably appointed with billiards room, card rooms, private dining rooms, well-stocked cigar counter and wine cellar, a fine collection of Canadian art and various amenities designed to soothe the nerves of the harried executive. Full course lunches and dinners were served in the main dining room, while sandwiches and simpler fare were available in the upstairs bar.

John waved at the doorman, signed me in as his guest and led me upstairs to the bar. We ordered grilled lobster and cheese sandwich, a National Club specialty. I asked John how things were going at the marina.

"Well, the boys have been a little slower than I hoped, but it's not really their fault. The new windshield only just arrived and they're putting it in this weekend. Everything else is ready."

"How d'you plan to get the boat to Georgian Bay?"

"Ah, that's where you come in. Figured the two of us could take her round by water."

"By *water?*"

John had mentioned earlier that the boat was on Rice Lake. I didn't know exactly where Rice Lake was, but I had a vague idea it was a good distance east of Toronto, and probably not far north of Lake Ontario. Georgian Bay, on the other hand, is part of Lake Huron, a 90-minute drive *northwest* of Toronto at its closest point and separated by 75 miles of solid land. So it seemed that John was making the preposterous suggestion that we navigate to Georgian Bay from Lake Ontario via Lakes Erie, St. Clair and Huron, a distance of nearly 700 miles, much of it over potentially stormy waters.

"Exactly where is this Rice Lake, anyway?"

"You mean you don't know? It's a large lake near Peterborough, about 75 miles northeast from here as the crow flies. Lots of Toronto people have their cottages there, you know," he added condescendingly.

"And just how do you plan to take the boat from there to Georgian Bay?"

"By the Trent System, of course."

I had forgotten about the Trent-Severn Waterway. This unsung series of lakes, rivers, canals and locks provides a direct navigational link over the high ridge of PreCambrian shield separating Lake Ontario from Lake Huron.

"Exactly what do you have in mind, John? Why can't we simply trailer the boat to Honey Harbour in Georgian Bay and have done with it?"

He looked at me as though I had betrayed a long-standing friendship.

"The Raven's too big and heavy to tow behind my wagon. I'd have to find a truck with a trailer hitch. Anyway," he looked out the window, "I thought it might be fun . . ."

"Listen, John, I'd love to go on that trip, you know I would, but I'm up to here with the Acme Data Systems deal. We file the red herring next week. I just can't swing it."

We left it that I would help him trailer the boat to Honey Harbour as soon as it was ready. We finished lunch in brittle silence.

᠊ᢣ ᢣ ᢣ

When I got back to the office, there was an urgent message from the lawyer. The owners of Acme had decided to postpone their initial public offering until the fall due to unsettled markets. My schedule was now wide open. But I demurred. Did I really want to expose myself to the vicissitudes of a several-day boat trip with John Frise, and all that might imply? I called John.

Frise was like a kid the night before Christmas. We left work early to buy charts.

ッ ッ ッ

Rice Lake, 20 miles long, marks the end of the Otonabee River and the start of the Trent River. Together these two rivers form the lower portion of the Trent-Severn Waterway that drains into Lake Ontario. The Trent (not to be part of our route on this occasion) starts at the east end of Rice Lake and drains out through various small lakes and 18 navigational locks all the way down to Lake Ontario. Our starting point would be the Otonabee River, at the west end of Rice Lake, right across from Gores Landing where the Raven now awaited us. We would proceed upstream from there.

On the charts our route looked like a maze of seemingly unconnected lakes and rivers. We would follow the Otonabee, a wide and meandering river, for about 25 miles, almost into Peterborough, before we entered the first lock. Shortly after Peterborough we would be lifted again, this time by the famous hydraulic lift lock which would send us clawing our way up a further series of locks all the way through the Kawartha Lakes to Balsam Lake, the high point of the system.

From Balsam we would descend in stages to Lake Simcoe and traverse the length of that very large lake before making our final run to Georgian Bay via Lake Couchiching and the Severn River. During the process we would climb 230 feet to Balsam Lake then descend 270 feet to Georgian Bay. We would pass through 25 locks including the Peterborough lift lock and the Big Chute marine railway near Gloucester Pool at the Georgian Bay end. In all, we would cover 175 miles.

"So that does it, Gordy," Frise slapped me on the back, "Georgian Bay in three days easy, sleep on board. We'll go to the office Monday morning, clear up odds and ends, then I'll pick you up at your place in the wagon around noon. We'll leave the wagon at Gores Landing, pick it up next week."

ッ ッ ッ

Monday dawned hot and muggy, the onset of the season's first heat wave. I swept the remnants of unfinished business into my top drawer and hurried home to finish packing. Di produced a sandwich, shaking her head.

"How you could take off and spend three days cooped up in a wooden cage with another lunatic like yourself is beyond me," she ventured kindly.

"Ah, it's for the adventure of it all, Disie, it's Because It's There. Something to talk about for years."

"Probably so, but not for the reasons you think. I doubt you'll even be speaking to each other three days from now."

I finished the sandwich and assembled my gear on the front step. A car screeched around the corner, some idiot in a little Ford Pinto with an enormous animal in the back seat. Then the Pinto lurched to a stop in front of our house and the horrible truth dawned on me. We were to make the trip in the Pinto and were to have the company of Frise's large black poodle.

I watched in disbelief as John unfolded himself from the tiny car. It seemed as though the dog occupied the entire remaining space. I had never seen such a large poodle.

"Meet Tramp, Wild Dog of the North."

"John, you can't be serious." I could see that Di was loving this. "Where's the wagon? Where's all our gear going to fit? Where am I going to fit? And what if that wretched creature has to pee between locks?"

"Never worry, my good man, there's lots of room in Libby's Pinto, and the Tramp is extremely intelligent and well trained." I looked at the animal dubiously as it munched on the passenger side headrest. "He'll be excellent company, and a good guard dog to boot." I had no doubt about the latter.

Just then our own black standard poodle emerged from the house. Sophie was a large dog but a Chihuahua compared to the behemoth inside the Pinto. Her timing was impeccable. Quickly seizing her advantage, she went on the offensive, circling the Pinto and executing a series of lightning fast rushes designed to goad and provoke. She succeeded beyond her wildest expectations. The Pinto shook and swayed like a helicopter trying to become airborn in a typhoon.

Somehow I managed to collar Sophie between rushes and dragged her snarling back to the house. When I emerged things had calmed down and Di was looking at me with her angelic smile.

"I am sure you boys are going to have the time of your lives," she said sweetly as she stuffed our food cooler into an already brimming trunk.

"G.G., why don't you get in front first and then I'll hand you your duffle bag. You won't mind travelling with it on your lap, I'm sure."

I rolled down the window and waved goodbye, remembering too late the soggy headrest. The trip to Rice Lake was a nightmare of contorted limbs and an overwhelming doggy presence, exacerbated by the humid weather and lack of air conditioning. I was never so happy as when we descended the final hill and pulled into the marina at Gores Landing. It was just 4:00 P.M.

John opened his door in a cloud of spent vapours and the bursting Tramp sprang from the back seat and disappeared over the hill, ignoring the repeated entreaties of his owner. So much for the well-trained part. John shrugged and we walked down to the docks to find the Raven.

There was no sign of her, and the place was strangely quiet.

"Funny," said John, "the boys said they'd put her in the water before they installed the windshield so that she could start to soak up. I guess they've taken her out on the lake for a spin. I didn't mention that we'd be coming."

"You mean *they don't even know we're coming?* They have no idea at all?"

"That's right. I thought it would be a nice surprise for them."

"John, I'll bet that boat isn't even in the water yet."

"Don't be ridiculous, man, of course it's in the water. Come on, I'll prove it to you." He led the way to a nearby boat shed and swung open the door. Then stepped back with his mouth agape. Behind the door was this large black boat with a whimsical canvas top like an English pram. The windshield was smashed and the top was torn, and the boat was covered with a thick layer of dust and swallow droppings. She hadn't even been touched. Leaning against the side was the new windshield.

"She's not very pretty," I ventured, walking around to the aft end. A low rumble emanated from somewhere within the shed. I thought I saw the twin exhausts move.

"What the hell was that?" I whispered, the hair on the back of my neck prickling.

"God*damn* them!" said John, ignoring my question, "They've been stringing me along all this time. Lies, lies and more lies. I'll sue them. Better still, I'll grind their gonads into the front steps of the Gores Landing post office!" And stomped off to find his intended victims.

There was no point accompanying him, so I took the opportunity to give the boat the once-over. I pulled myself up onto one of the trestles and climbed aboard. The first thing I noticed was the honesty of the woodwork inside: exposed oak ribs and mahogany lapstrake from the gunwales to the flooring. I lifted the engine box to see beneath the floorboards and noted the identical hull treatment clear down to the keel. What you sees is what you gets.

I paused to take in the overall layout. She was an open day cruiser with a cuddy forward and the wheel approximately amidships, an unusually modern setup for a vessel of that vintage. The wheel was seamanlike: heavy duty chromed brass with man-sized mahogany spokes. On the instrument panel was a plaque: "Century – Thoroughbred of Boats." The mahogany door to the cuddy cabin also had solid-looking chromed brass fittings. The little cabin itself had scarcely enough room to sleep two, but the V-bunks looked comfortable enough. I put my hand on the varnished dash and felt a responsive tingle, a warm sense of belonging, of comfortable familiarity.

I peered through the broken windshield at the deck and laughed. The previous owner had for practical reasons applied treated canvas, painted off-white, over the original pinstripe mahogany deck. He had also painted the rim of the round hatch cover the same colour, giving it the jaunty appearance of a country one-holer. The barn swallows had evidently taken the hint.

I climbed back down and crawled underneath the boat to check the hull for dry rot. I took out my penknife and poked the tip of the blade gently into the wood around the stem and the forward part of the keel – a vulnerable location – and noted with satisfaction the firm resistance to the blade and the crisp withdrawal. I tested the keel around the shaft, the skeg and the rudder, and was just finishing off around the transom when I was rudely grabbed from behind.

"What the hell are you doing?" Frise was highly agitated.

"Just checking for dry rot. I'm happy to say she seems –"

"For Chrissakes, Green, I've already bought the boat so what difference does it make? Just don't go round sticking a knife into her. It lets the moisture in and then the paint will blister."

"Okay, John, lighten up. I was only doing what I do to my own boat." That bit about letting the moisture in was news to me, but I held my peace. John was understandably bent out of shape at the turn of events, but less understandably he was taking it out on me. Fortunately at that instant a boat pulled up to the docks, and when John saw that the driver was none other than the marina owner he strode off to do battle.

There was a lot of shouting and I couldn't make out much of what was said except for the occasional phrase like pure fabrication and legal liability and senior executive giving up his valuable time (presumably me). Then they started walking toward me and I could hear clearly.

"All right, then, Mr. Frise, we'll launch her right away and put her in the slings overnight, and we'll install the windshield first thing in the morning . . ."

"I should think so."

". . . and we'll forget about all the other work. But she still won't be ready for you to take out for a couple of days. You'd be crazy if you tried to run her before that. She needs two full days to soak up."

"We'll see about that."

I took a deep breath and looked up at the incongruous toilet seat. Tramp appeared out of nowhere and lifted his leg against the trestle. Another faint rumble issued from within.

3

A Spoke in My Fly

THE NORTHUMBERLAND HEIGHTS Country Inn sits on a height of land surrounded by rolling hills just northeast of Cobourg, about ten miles from Gores Landing. Our table in the dining room looked out over Lake Ontario. John had recovered completely from his earlier vapours and talked enthusiastically of leaving before noon next day.

"John, you're nuts. We take off tomorrow, she'll leak like a sieve. She'll be too heavy to handle. All those extra stresses on the frame. We'll be far better off waiting the extra day."

"No way, can't afford the time. We'll just have to keep pumping her out." He had a simple answer for everything. "Ah, waiter," he signalled to the surprised owner, "be a good man and bring me another doggy bag, will you?"

I gave it one more try. "At least wait until noon. Let her soak up those few extra hours. We're not in that desperate a hurry."

"Relax, Gordy, everything'll be okay. And listen. I'm sorry I bit your head off in the boat shed. You're such a pompous prick sometimes. Now let's get an early bed. Want to get going as soon as she's ready."

We fed Tramp from the doggy bags and put him to bed for the night in the back seat of the Pinto.

⚓ ⚓ ⚓

Tramp loped over fields and through woods in the early morning dew chasing real and imagined rabbits, covering huge distances. His energy was incredible. I wondered how he would take to being cooped up for three days in a wooden prison.

Back at the marina the new windshield was taking longer to install than anticipated. This frustrated John, but the extra hours were a blessing. The work was completed just before noon.

"I tell you, boys, I'll not take any responsibility for this. You should be leaving her in the slings another day." The marina owner shook his head as we loaded in the last of our gear. "Look at the water inside," he said, "it's just pouring in."

At least he had cleaned her up a bit. Now that the frivolous pram top was down, the Raven looked almost dignified.

We jumped in and John fired up the engine. I listened to the deep-throated growl of the Interceptor's eight cylinders, strangely reminiscent of that earlier rumble. The bilge pump now just kept up with the inrushing waters and the Raven floated easily at her normal waterline. Tramp was brought aboard, a reluctant passenger. I held him firmly by the collar and smiled thinly at the small group that had gathered to send us off.

Someone pushed us out. Suddenly Tramp gave a tremendous lurch and broke free of my grip, easily clearing the widening gap between boat and dock, and headed for the parking lot and the Pinto, his new home.

"For Crissakes, Green, one lousy job and you screw up!" Frise threw the boat into reverse and gunned the engine. Unfortunately my friend had not yet learned the finer points of handling a larger, single-screw craft. The Raven dug in and carved a reverse doughnut at full throttle right into the dock, scattering the crowd. I jumped off with the bowline and strained to avoid a dunking as the boat bounced back and tried to take me with it, then thrust the line into the hands of a surprised onlooker and ran off to retrieve the dog.

John was humiliated and in foul humour. He grabbed Tramp by the collar as I jumped down into the boat.

"Don't stomp on the floorboards like that," he hissed, "you're likely to break through." Again I bit my tongue.

We headed out past Black Island toward the centre of the lake. John gradually opened the throttle until the Raven purred along at 3600 RPM, I guessed about 25 knots. The boat ran smoothly and had power to spare. The tensions began to evaporate. It was just 2:00 P.M., ample time to cover the 25 miles to Peterborough before evening.

The Otonabee River empties into Rice Lake in a large delta, the main channel running between two spits projecting half a mile out into the lake. As we slowed to pass between the entrance buoys, the boat started to wallow seasickeningly. John cut the throttle and water rushed over the floorboards. The bilge pump was going full tilt.

"Holy shit, we're sinking!"

"Maybe not," I said, mindful of my own experience with the leaky Hunter. "She runs bow high, so when you open her up all the water rushes to the stern, away from the bilge pump. Meanwhile more water is being forced through the loose planks at the front. This'll probably continue until she has a real chance to tighten up."

Three or four minutes of pumping confirmed my assessment. After that we established a pattern of cruising for several minutes and then stopping to pump her out. Running the pump while under way was futile and would have burned out the impellor.

"Green I have to admit you know a bit about boats even if you're an obnoxious over-educated stuffed shirt." High praise indeed from John Frise. The prospects for a harmonious trip took a turn for the better.

We were now passing through movie-set Louisiana bayou country – swampy plains and muddy tributaries through which the wide and lazy Otonabee wound its way. A large marshy tributary appeared off the port bow, on the chart marked appropriately Steamboat Creek. Any minute now I expected to encounter a sternwheeler round the next bend, Al Jolson on the bridge and the leadsman at the rail calling "mark twain!." The setting was intensified by a number of small shacks scattered along the river banks, their occupants nearly all what we then called Blacks. (We subsequently learned that generations of these families had been driving up from the Detroit area each year to rent the same shanty for a week's fishing.) Now the steamy weather and the endless flatlands transported us to another era and another part of the continent.

We followed along in this twilight zone for several miles, stopping every now and then to relieve the Raven of her watery burden. A bridge came into view, the first sign of civilization since we left the lake.

"What's that bridge?"

"Let's see . . . ah, Bensfort Bridge, one of only two bridges across the river between Rice Lake and Peterborough. That means we must be nearly half way to Peterborough."

"Great. Hey, Gordy, why don't you take over for a while? She seems very comfortable at about 3600 RPM."

Delighted and surprised, I took the wheel and my spirits soared. I was at one with the boat – felt I had known her all my life. I could feel her throbbing twin exhausts through my fingertips, her smooth power, her impulsive need to go faster. I throttled back to get a feel for the controls, then briefly increased the revs to 4200 before pulling her back to cruising speed. I was amazed at how light and responsive she was.

We passed under Bensfort Bridge and came to an S-bend in the river, first a gentle curve to the right and then a sharp turn to the left where the river narrowed. I noticed how eagerly the Raven took the starboard leg: she almost seemed to know where we were heading. But when I straightened out and prepared for the tighter turn to the left I felt a new resistance. It was as though there was a large wave in front of the port bow pushing us away from our intended course. I started to rein in this balky thoroughbred, but the more I pulled to the left *the harder she wanted to turn right!*

Now the headstrong creature had the bit firmly in her teeth. She continued to strain against me, listing to starboard, and before I knew it the left-hand curve was upon us. I swung the wheel hard to the left but the Raven shot like a bullet to the right, straight at the nearby bank. At the last moment I cut the throttle and slammed her into full reverse. She screamed, dug in, and came to a stop not 25 feet from disaster.

John looked at me in stunned silence.

"Are you out of your mind? What in hell's name were you doing?"

"Jesus," I croaked, "I turned her full to the left and she shot off in the opposite direction! *Jesus!*"

I didn't realize it then, but I had just experienced my first clash of wills with the Raven. Now I knew what the previous owner had meant when he said he couldn't handle her any more. But still I felt a rush.

John lifted the engine hatch and saw that the water level was easily a foot below the floorboards. The steering problem wasn't caused by inertia from the volume of water in the bilge – there just wasn't enough water for that. He leaned over the transom and asked me to turn the wheel full one way and then the other.

"Rudder's working fine," he said, "so that's not the problem either. You just didn't have the wheel over as far as you thought. There's no way she could have veered over like that on her own."

"Dammit, John, listen. I'm not imagining things. She didn't just pull to starboard, she jumped there. And I had the wheel turned over hard to port."

He came forward and grabbed the wheel, firmly easing me aside. "Here, look, Gordy," he said, standing against the wheel and pointing at his crotch, "Right there, against my fly. See? It means you caught one of the spokes in your fly. You just *think* you had the wheel turned all the way, but it was jammed in your crotch, man. No wonder you had that idiotic grin on your face!"

Vintage Frise. I had to laugh. Anyone could tell there was something dangerously wrong with the boat. I knew I would soon be vindicated – but meanwhile John would be doing all the piloting.

Before long we passed under the second bridge at Wallace Point. Signs of civilization started to appear on both sides of the river – first roads, then houses and factories. As we approached the town of Peterborough we slowed to enter Lock 19 at Scott's Mills.

꙳ ꙳ ꙳

The events that took place at Lock 19, etched forever in my memory, were related more to John's lack of experience in handling a single-engine inboard than to the recent near-disaster at Bensfort Bridge. Fast single-engine inboards with shallow skegs often yaw, or veer off course, at low speeds because the steering depends mostly on the thrust of the propeller against the tiny rudder. At low speeds, that thrust is insufficient to provide directional stability.

Experienced inboarders know this and utilize the propeller's natural sideways thrust, or torque, to counter such perverse behaviour. But John was not an experienced inboarder, and unfortunately for him, among boats destined for poor low-speed handling, none was more qualified than the Raven. Her hull was shaped like a rubber duck, and her lily-dip rudder and shallow skeg provided less directional stability at low speed than a duck's tail feathers.

Lock 19 is nestled against the left bank of the river at the end of a noisy foaming weir. The lock gates had just opened to disgorge a large cruiser and a sailboat. John gently put the Raven in gear and headed toward the lock when suddenly, with no warning, we made a sideways lurch for the cruiser. I shouted to John and he pulled the wheel first one way and then the other. We zig-zagged right under the cruiser's bow, missing it by inches. A group gathered at the cruiser's rail to watch as we skittered crabwise past the lock entrance and shot into the frothing water below the weir.

Muttering obscenities, John powered a large circle and lined up carefully to resume his approach. But as soon as he slowed down he lost control again. With an exasperated curse he gunned the boat full throttle straight at the open lock gates. Boats and astonished onlookers blurred by as we shot into the bowels of the dripping chamber. At the last minute John flung the Raven into reverse, sending me crashing against the seats and Tramp in a self-assisted trajectory. I don't know which end of the leash was the more surprised. The leash jerked out of my hand and Tramp managed to claw desperately at the lip of the wall before gaining a foothold and disappearing in the direction of the weir.

I tried to grab one of the mooring cables with the boathook but missed. Our momentum carried us crossways to the centre of the lock, out of reach of the cables. The lockkeeper scratched his head. John appeared unconcerned.

"Miscalculated slightly on the approach, ha-ha. No problem, get it right next time."

He didn't even notice Tramp was missing.

The lockkeeper made a megaphone with his hands. "Dog's tryin' to cross the weir. Hurry and get over so's I can close the gates." We did, and rose with the water. Soon we could see Tramp on the other side of the lock by the edge of the weir, but the dog couldn't hear John yelling at him over the roar of the water.

The lockkeeper opened the gates and motioned us out. We wanted to go out on the weir to retrieve the dog, so we just sat there. He kept waving us out with increasing agitation. Three boats were waiting, sounding their horns. Finally the lockkeeper strode out onto the weir, grabbed the recalcitrant Tramp by the collar with an exaggerated motion and dragged him back.

Still we had to run the gauntlet of the other boats. I suggested we start by pushing the boat across to the other side of the lock before starting the motor.

This worked well. Emboldened, I ventured a couple of helpful pointers on handling inboards.

"Funny thing about my Hunter, John, for some reason she seems to track better at low speeds if I leave her in neutral . . ."

"Oh sure. And I suppose she steers by Divine Guidance."

"John, I mean it. I keep her on course by nudging her in and out of gear. Combination of thrust and torque."

"Torque schmorque, you Harvard MBAs are all the same. Who's the engineer around here anyway? The basic difference between your boat and mine is that yours has a primitive mechanical clutch, while the sophisticated Raven here has a velvet-smooth Borg-Warner hydromatic drive that wasn't designed to take your crude in-again-out-again treatment like some horny rabbit."

Our intellectual discourse continued against a background of blaring horns.

"So what we're going to do is to exit the same way we came in. I'll be driving the boat in gear and steering with the steering wheel, just like a car. You have two simple duties, Green – boathook and dog. Just keep us and the bloody hound off the walls and away from the other boats and we'll do fine. Now if you're ready, you over-educated slob, kindly push us off so we get to the Holiday Inn before the bar closes."

Boathook and dog. Boathook and dog. I held Tramp's lead firmly in one hand and pushed off gingerly with the other, careful to keep the boat straight. John engaged the drive and the stern kicked back hard into the wall.

"Damn. Push her out harder!"

I did, and we shot right across the lock to the opposite wall. I braced myself for another verbal onslaught, but at that moment John accelerated sharply and I lost my balance and let go of everything. I lunged for the disappearing lead with one hand, bringing the dog up short again, then twisted around to fend us off with the boathook. We ricocheted once and then catapulted out past the waiting boats and under the bridge at Highway 7.

"See?" shouted John, "Nothing to it."

⚓ ⚓ ⚓

We passed under a swinging railway bridge and out onto Little Lake, the broadening of the Otonabee around which the town of Peterborough is built. There a magnificent sight greeted us. The fountain in the middle of the lake is a famous Peterborough landmark. I had often seen it from the air on flights to and from Montreal, but up close it was far more impressive. It seemed to soar hundreds of feet into the air.

"There's the Holiday Inn, John, just to the left of the fountain. I can see the dock, and I'm sure the bar's still open."

4

Vindication at Hell's Gate

WE BREAKFASTED early and hurried down to the dock, our footsteps loud in the morning stillness. A startled heron gave raucous complaint and departed on ponderous wings. We climbed aboard the Raven and checked the bilge – completely dry. Little Lake beckoned, and beyond it the canal.

The towering structure of the lift lock loomed before us. Completed in 1904, it is one of the world's largest hydraulic lift locks, raising and lowering boats 65 feet in a single operation. It took eight years to build, and its substructure contains 26,000 cubic yards of concrete – a huge monolithic mass even when compared to today's megaprojects. It replaces the work of four conventional locks that would have been required to bypass the Otonabee rapids above Peterborough.

From our vantage downstream, the structure looked like two monstrous garage hoists working in counterpoint. Atop each hoist was a tank 140 feet long, 33 feet wide and 9 feet deep, commodious enough for several large boats. As one tank was lowered the other was raised. When each chamber had reached its final position, its double lock gates were opened to allow equalization of water levels, and an exchange of boats took place. The cycle was then repeated in reverse.

John Frise, P. Eng., was absorbed by this engineering marvel. He had read that the lifting operation is powered entirely by the natural forces of gravity. Each tank is lifted and lowered by a gigantic piston, or hydraulic ram, seven and a half feet in diameter, interconnected one to the other by conduits with shutoff valves. The descending chamber carries more water and so is heavier than the one being lifted. This places pressure through the conduit on the other ram causing it to rise, just like a garage hoist. When the tanks are actually six inches short of their final destination the operator closes the valves to stop the lifting action. He then opens the lock gates, and water rises in the upper chamber and spills out of the lower chamber to adjust to the level of the surrounding water. The combined effect of this inward and outward spillage is that the previously lighter upper tank now has 144 tons more water than the lower one.

In accordance with Archimedes' bathtub principle, the new weight of each tank remains constant regardless of the size and number of boats that subsequently move into or out of each. Thus, when the lock gates are finally closed and the conduit valves opened – *Eureka!* – 144 tons of pressure are exerted on the lower ram, causing it to rise while the other falls. The lifting action itself takes only 90 seconds; the entire cycle is completed in ten minutes.

John shook his head in wonderment at the structure surrounding us and was oblivious to our crabwise entrance to the chamber. I hooked a mooring cable as he threw the boat into reverse and the stern kicked out. I managed to hold on to the boat hook as Tramp sat docilely at the end of his lead.

"Ah, Green, we travel a waterway steeped in history. Took them nearly 100 years to complete this canal system."

He had been reading a book on the building of the Trent-Severn Waterway.

"Compare that to the Erie Canal which was finished in only eight years, or the Suez in ten. Even the Panama only took 30 years."

I was interested in the history all right, but was more fascinated to see how the lift lock mechanism worked. The gates closed and we started our ascent. It was like riding a quiet and efficient elevator.

"Political indecision dragged on for years," John continued, waving in the general direction of the canal ahead, "then just as things were set to go, along came the railway and removed all the incentive to complete the project. First locks were built in the early 1830s, but the final connection at Couchiching was only completed in 1920. What a feat! Those early engineers certainly knew how to play their slide rules. No computers or fancy calculators for them!"

The lift stopped and the water rose its requisite six inches as we prepared to leave.

"This time, Green, don't let the stern kick back. Give her a good shove. Don't baby her."

I shoved firmly, and we swung right across again. "Not *that* hard, dammit!" I braced myself for the inevitable lurch as he gunned her away.

It was still early morning and a steamy haze hung low over the narrow canal. We had to slow to three knots, the speed limit imposed to minimize bank erosion. Mercifully this was just fast enough to forestall the dreaded yaw, but I could sense John's impatience. We hoped to spend the night on Lake Simcoe aboard the Raven before making the final run to Georgian Bay the next day. There were 20 locks and untold lakes between here and Simcoe.

The canal widened as we entered a small man-made lake which led us back to the Otonabee. Soon the attractive modern buildings of Trent University passed by our port bow. We continued north through several rural locks and then came once more to a built-up area.

"Where are we?" John cut the throttle as we approached another lock.

"Lakefield," I said, consulting the chart. "The canal goes right through the centre of town and then takes us out onto Lake Katchewanooka. After that we should make up some time as we'll be travelling mostly through lakes. But John, honest to God we have to stop at this lock to pee the dog. He's bursting."

"Pee, schmee, Tramp can bloody well wait for the next lock. He's got a strong constitution and an even stronger bladder. Let's go!"

He gunned the boat sharply as we approached the lock.

"FRISE SLOW DOWN!"

The 16-foot high lock gates flew by as John jammed the Raven into screaming reverse, launching Tramp on yet another bid for freedom.

This time I had his number, but unfortunately his lead was in my left hand and he was headed right. He landed with a great splash off the starboard rail and continued to pull ferociously as I lunged across with my other hand to hook the cable. Thus trussed like an Egyptian mummy, I already felt seriously compromised when Frise chose that moment to gun the motor. The stern shot out and the rubber handle parted with a loud thwock, sending the boathook flying in an arc back to the lock wall where it bounced once before disappearing into the depths. I fell hard against the gunwales.

"Hey, what's going on?" Frise heard the splash. "Look out, Green, for crying out loud, the cable, man, grab the cable!" We drifted toward the centre of the lock.

"Where's the boathook? What have you been doing, flying in outer space? I mean I just can't believe you let go the bloody wall again."

I held out the useless rubber handle and nodded in the direction of the spluttering dog.

"Jesus," he muttered.

⚓ ⚓ ⚓

Tramp thrashed mightily with his front paws and it took our combined strength to wrestle the sodden creature back on board. As John turned to put the boat in gear the dog jumped on the engine box and shook himself vigorously. John's furious yell dispelled the last of my self control. The curmudgeonly boat, the sore arms, the verbal abuse, and now Tramp's exquisite revenge for the denied pee break – all erupted in blissful therapeutic release: a serious bout of uncontrollable, helpless laughter.

My audience was not amused.

⚓ ⚓ ⚓

We tied up at a nearby dock. The lockkeeper had the good grace to look away. Perhaps he had something wrong with his eye, for he kept wiping it. Also he may have had some kind of emotional disorder, for each time he tried to give directions to the nearest marine supply store he choked off in mid-sentence, shoulders shaking.

We soon returned with a new aluminum boathook (handle securely taped), sandwiches from a local lunch counter, and an emptied Tramp. I gave the lockkeeper a knowing nod as we pushed off.

⚓ ⚓ ⚓

Katchewanooka is a narrow lake, an extension of the Otonabee River. The north end led us into a channel which emptied from Clear Lake.

Here the scenery changed. Beside us a large weir thundered – the head of the Otonabee watershed.

We were now entering the Kawartha Lakes district, marked by massive granite outcroppings and wind-blown pines: the area where the waterway becomes a series of zig-zag lines joining a patchwork of seemingly unrelated lakes through haphazard low spots in the PreCambrian Shield, reputedly the oldest rock in the world.

For the first time since Rice Lake we felt we were on open water. It was close to noon, and the morning haze had given way to blue skies, with only a few storm clouds on the northern horizon. The Raven showed her paces as the Interceptor growled along at 4300 RPM, close to 30 knots. Frise sang at the top of his voice between bites of sandwich, portly Wagnerian frame atop muscular legs, silver hair in the wind. I knew exactly how he felt – I had experienced that same euphoria just before Bensfort Bridge.

Clear Lake merges at the north end with popular Stony Lake, well named for its many perilous shoals. There our course would take us through a tight left turn around a prominent headland and then into an infamous shoal-infested channel called Hell's Gate.

I had spread the open chart on the engine cover and weighted it with the boat hook, and was trying to pick out the first red marker.

"I think that's the marker there, John, about two o'clock, quarter of a mile ahead." He nodded and altered course.

We flew past the buoy and continued toward Sherin Island and the entrance to Hell's Gate. As we started to make a gentle sweep to the left in preparation for the sharp turn, the note of the engine changed, imperceptibly at first but then into a distinct snarl. I felt the Raven taughten, and then she started to lean to starboard, away from the turn. I instinctively grabbed Tramp's collar.

I looked at Frise. He was struggling with the wheel, no doubt about it. A shoal barely broke the surface to the right, about fifty yards ahead. I shouted a warning but he had already seen the shoal and was hauling the wheel hard to the left. Predictably, the Raven bolted straight for the shoal. He frantically threw her into reverse. The engine screamed, the bow rose out of the water like a scene from *Jaws*, and the boathook nearly impaled Tramp on the cabin door. We reared terrifyingly for a moment before subsiding, the stem softly bumping the rock. The chart fluttered harmlessly over the side. Frise slumped over the wheel.

"She did it," he gasped, "My God, Gordy, she really did it!"

Vindication is sweet, but we were both truly shaken. I recovered the boathook and fished out the sodden chart, searching for an appropriate comment. On balance, I thought it best not to ask John if he would like me to help him untangle the pesky spoke from his fly.

5

Gathering Storm

A CHASTENED John Frise gingerly picked his way through the Hell's Gate obstacle course. He was so crestfallen I felt sorry for him. I spread the chart out to dry and cheerfully called out place names. The original settlers had a fine sense of humour: we were passing Devil's Elbow and Hell's Gate on our way to Hurricane Bend between Hurricane Point and Butcher's Island. By bizarre contrast, the large island around which this whole mariner's nightmare was draped was Fairy Lake Island, while just off to our left was Fiji and, farther ahead, Lovesick Lake.

We could see the white water of Burleigh Falls at the end of Burleigh Bay. The storm clouds to the north had grown dark and taller, the air heavier. John approached the lock with uncharacteristic diffidence. He slipped the Raven into neutral and we didn't yaw at all. I feigned preoccupation with the charts.

"This is one big lock, Frisbee. It raises us 24 feet past the falls. Now we're into that crazy quiltwork portion of the Kawarthas. We'll be zig-zagging between lakes for quite a while."

Frise grunted. I reached out and easily hooked a mooring cable. Tramp just sat there panting.

I wasn't accustomed to such tranquillity. I made up for it on departure by pushing out too softly. The stern kicked back and I had to lunge with the boathook to keep us off the wall.

"For the love of my maiden aunt, Green, push harder! You're not playing with your little rubber duckey in the bathtub, or with anything else for that matter."

That felt better.

⚓ ⚓ ⚓

The air was heavy as we came to the lock between Lower Buckhorn and Buckhorn Lake. An intense sun bore down, but the sky to the north was now completely dark, and occasionally we heard a distant rumble. Ahead, white water marked the rapids below the weir.

We passed under a bridge and entered the lock chamber. A row of inscrutable fishermen sat behind us on the edge of the bridge under large conical straw hats, long bamboo poles pointed towards us, bare feet dangling, figurines from a Willow Pattern china setting. We waved but they just sat expressionless.

The water level rose and brought our backs closer to the fishermen. Then the gates opened and John started the engine. Ahead lay 200 yards of narrow exit channel along which several waiting boats were tied.

I gave a healthy shove off the wall just as the engine stalled. For several precious seconds all that Frise could elicit from the Raven was an impotent weah-weah-weah from the starter.

"Damned airlock in the fuel line," he muttered, pumping the throttle rapidly as we continued to swing in a great arc. I could feel the eyes on the bridge.

At last the Interceptor sputtered and caught, and Frise cleared the carburettors with a roar of belching black smoke. By this time we had turned full round to face our audience.

"Head down now, Green," Frise hissed between clenched teeth. "Shit. No room to turn here. Have to back out."

I couldn't believe what was happening. Frise really was determined to back out. Eyes down and whistling a tuneless refrain, he put the boat in reverse, although we both knew that in this mode the Raven had absolutely no steerage. But pride was at stake here.

"Act nonchalant," he whispered out of the corner of his mouth. "Just keep us away from the sides."

He looked neither right nor left. We backed down the narrow channel as I dashed from side to side fending us off like a ball in a pinball machine. More spectators appeared. It seemed the gauntlet would never end.

At last the canal widened and there was enough room to turn around and John carved a tight circle and we roared out onto Buckhorn Lake and stopped there and hooted and hollered and high-fived and danced a Scottish reel, two teenagers pulling off an illicit prank. In the background the Chinese hats sat motionless and serene.

᭒ ᭒ ᭒

We were now in the heart of the Kawarthas, the scenery out of a tourist brochure. The gathering storm clouds still held back and the water reflected the intense blues and greens of sky and trees as we passed under the bridge at Shannon Narrows and headed out onto Pigeon Lake.

"Next stop the town of Bobcaygeon," said Frise. "The lock there between Sturgeon Lake and Pigeon Lake was the first one built on the entire system – 1833. Locals grew tired of the political wrangling and decided to build the weir and lock themselves. It's still the original design."

We took the diversion past Big Bob Channel and entered the six-foot lock. John now routinely let the Raven drift in neutral on our approach.

A towering cloudbank swallowed the sun as we rounded the southern point of V-shaped Sturgeon Lake and headed north toward the town of Fenelon Falls. The black base of the cloudbank was lit with occasional flickers, and increased rumbling gave notice anew of celestial indigestion.

We tied up at the town dock to relieve Tramp and buy provisions for our next two shipboard meals. We left the top down.

"If the weather'll just hold off till we reach Simcoe it can rain all it wishes," said John prophetically as we rose through the 26-foot lock. "We should be good and watertight in the bunks up forward."

The threatening storm added urgency to our passage. We flew across Cameron Lake and entered the short canal that marks the final step to the summit at Balsam Lake. There we were greeted by a large sign posting the three-knot speed limit.

"Don't pay any attention to that," said Frise breezily. "It's only intended for the larger cruisers, you know, the ones that throw up a huge wake." He accelerated to five knots, creating a tidal wave that flirted with the top of the canal banks.

"Hey, careful, there's a lock ahead."

The lockkeeper looked at us accusingly as we entered the chamber. Our backwash caught up with us and threw us alternately into and away from the wall. The waves prevented him from closing the gates, and he struggled with his giant wheel for several seconds before the backpressure subsided enough to allow the gates to come together. He glowered down at us but Frise was oblivious. As soon as the gates opened he gunned the Raven and we headed up the canal toward the town of Rosedale at the entrance to Balsam Lake. I didn't care to look back.

Weather-wise we still held our own. The late afternoon sky was shot with red as we rounded Grand Island on Balsam Lake and headed toward the entrance of the canal. The lake shimmered in the changing light, a beautiful body of water, deservedly treasured by cottagers and tourists alike; a fitting place for us to bid farewell to the Kawarthas.

The reappearance of the speed limit as we entered the canal was the final straw. Frise accelerated to about eight knots, the point of maximum wake for the Raven (which threw progressively less wake beyond that speed), and that was when peculiar things began to happen. First I noticed a strange slurping sound and looked back and saw our wake washing clean over the banks of the canal, inundating shrubs and rocks in its path. Ahead, the level of the water sank several inches as the Raven's screw sucked great quantities of canal and threw them behind.

Then we rounded a bend and headed toward Mitchell Lake, the smaller of two artificial lakes created by the canal. Ahead was a fisherman bent over, changing his worm. Poor fellow, his back was to the canal and he hadn't even seen or heard us.

"My God, John!"

"I know. Don't even look."

I didn't – couldn't. But the scream and the stream of invective left little to the imagination.

Canal bank dwellers aside, I was genuinely concerned about erosion. I watched one bank carefully as the water washed cleanly over it. It looked pretty solid to me. The canal had been around a long time, and over the years it had doubtless seen far worse. But I was just rationalizing.

Soon we came to the Kirkfield lift lock, similar to its counterpart in Peterborough but much smaller. We slowed to three knots and innocently drifted in. From our higher vantage point atop the lift we could see Canal Lake stretching before us, and beyond it Talbot River leading to Lake Simcoe. We could just make out Simcoe spread out on the horizon. Storm clouds were building once more, and the lake looked looked dark and forbidding.

⚓ ⚓ ⚓

The first drops of rain hit the windshield as we entered Talbot River – great pregnant globules full of portent. There was no wind, but staccato flashes over Lake Simcoe put us on notice that this time we were not likely to escape. We stopped to put up the top.

"We can't make it all the way to Simcoe today anyway, John," I said, mindful of the lake's reputation for sudden storms. I folded up the still dry chart and stowed it. "Two more locks on the Talbot should do it, then we can find somewhere to batten down. River's quite wide by the entrance to the canal, good for anchorage. The final three locks in the canal will be a snap in the morning."

John grunted reluctant acceptance. The rain and the impending darkness had taken the edge off his enthusiasm.

⚓ ⚓ ⚓

Donning raingear, we entered a secluded bay just short of the canal entrance and dropped anchor. An overhanging willow served as our bow line cleat. By loosening the anchor line we could gain easy access to the shore – something that Tramp sorely needed. It was nearly dark by the time we had completed preparations, and by now it was seriously raining.

The Raven's torn top provided scant protection over the cheeses and cold meats we spread out on the engine box, but farther forward we managed to stay dry. I balanced a flashlight on the dash to relieve the dreary scene. We opened a beer.

"Relax, Frisbee, we're on schedule. Final three locks and out onto Lake Simcoe in the morning easy before you're even awake."

A loud thunderclap drowned out his response. The rain intensified. Tramp crawled behind John's legs, trembling pathetically. Some Wild Dog of the North.

By our second beer the storm was all around us. The wind screamed and drove the rain in horizontal sheets. Crackling peals of thunder chased stuttering forks and brightnesses across the roiling sky. Crash followed flash with growing urgency until the explosions seemed right overhead. We wondered why we had chosen to park ourselves right beneath that willow tree.

Then a hand reached down and switched on all the lights. Dazzling daylight flooded us as a simultaneous detonation rocked the boat. The air buzzed, rank with an acrid smell, and our hair stood on end. Tramp scratched frantically at the cabin door.

I opened the door and the dog rushed in and cowered on the bunks. Despite the histrionics we seemed to have avoided a direct hit, but it must have been close.

The storm left as quickly as it had arrived. One minute we were embroiled in this scene from Hades, the next the wind had dropped and gentle drum rolls receded into the distance, a Beethovian Shepherds' Hymn. Tramp emerged to clean up the soggy bread and cheese left on the engine box. We prepared to retire.

The toilet seat hatch had done its job. True to John's prediction the bunks stayed dry through all the driving rain. But the atmosphere inside the little cabin was appalling. We opened the door and hatch wide and lay on top of our sleeping bags, perspiring. Often a storm will clear the air, but this night there wasn't a breath of wind, and the air hung hot and heavy.

"That was quite a storm," I said, not ready yet for sleep, "I didn't enjoy that at all."

"It's all to do with the contours," said John, tracing lines on the ceiling. "Look at a map and you can see that Lake Simcoe is just an extension of the Georgian Bay."

He always put the "the" before Georgian Bay, just like the oldtimers. It reminded him of the halcyon days when the Bay was remote, accessible only to the privileged few, among which he counted himself.

"The Bruce Peninsula and the ridge of hills around Collingwood deflect the weather straight at Simcoe," he continued, yawning. "The air travels hundreds of miles over Lake Huron gathering moisture and cooling off, and then it hits the land, causing thermal upheaval and erratic precipitation. That's why Barrie is the snow belt of Ontario in the winter and has these violent storms in the summer. There's even the occasional tornado. And remember Hurricane Hazel that wiped out

Holland Landing in 1954? That came in the same way. Ah, well, Gordy, no more storms tonight. Tomorrow the Georgian Bay. Sweet dreams."

⇜ ⇜ ⇜

The whine of a dentist's drill invaded my exposed ear. I swatted hard and succeeded in setting up a loud ringing in both ears. This seemed to attract half the mosquito population of eastern Lake Simcoe. Tramp whimpered in his sleep and Frise began to snore.

I burrowed deep into my sleeping bag and left only a tiny hole to breathe through. I nearly suffocated. Meanwhile the wooden hull reverberated as though the string section of the Toronto Symphony Orchestra were tuning up inside the cabin. Blissfully unaware of the bloodthirsty marauders, my two cabin mates wheezed and rasped atop John's sleeping bag. Why was such succulent accessibility totally ignored by the little vampires? The injustice of it all and the intimacy of our quarters kept me awake through most of the night.

6

Deliverance

A SOLO MALE VOICE, not very tuneful, replaced the string section. I opened one eye and shut it again quickly. Frise was out there somewhere brushing his teeth, gargling, hawking over the stern.

I pulled myself out of the cramped quarters and painfully emerged, blinking at the surrounding scene. Broken branches, leaves and debris were everywhere. The tree we had tied up to was intact, but across the river, not a hundred yards away, a large willow had been split down the middle, one charred half lying on the ground. I scratched at my itching face and neck.

"Morning, Jake," I said, "Sleep well?"

An affimative grunt.

"No trouble from mosquitoes or anything like that?"

Negative grunt.

I indicated the broken tree. "Guess we were pretty lucky last night. Must have come close."

He nodded, gargled and spat.

This one-sided conversation wasn't going anywhere so I turned to my ablutions. I couldn't find my razor so I borrowed John's. It acted like a cheese grater.

"John, I need a new blade. This one's pretty far gone."

"Ah my good fellow," he said, suddenly recovering his voice and gesturing at the surrounding countryside, "Behold the devastation that surrounds us. We have to learn to conserve what little is left on this planet. The blade you are using is almost new – I changed it only last month. You should learn to suffer a little in the interests of conservation. Why discard a perfectly good blade so early in its tender career?"

It was too early in the morning for that kind of gibberish. The man either had a rawhide face or his whiskers were made of cheese. I resigned myself to a bloodied face.

❧ ❧ ❧

The northeast wind sent low clouds scudding across Lake Simcoe. Close to shore the water was protected, but farther out large whitecaps portended a rough crossing.

Our intended course took us out onto the open lake to clear Mara Point and then north toward the town of Orillia, home of Stephen Leacock and Gordon Lightfoot. I mused over the relative endurance of these two creative geniuses as we rounded the point and turned to face the weather head on. Both local heroes had written of the tyranny of the open waters. Refrains from Lightfoot's *Wreck of the Edmund Fitzgerald* ran through my head as I tried to remember whether anyone actually got hurt in Leacock's *Sinking of the Mariposa Belle*. Large rollers frothed and pounded at our starboard bow. The Raven rode the waves well but we soon discovered she had no bow flare to shed the water. As soon as we cut into a wave, a wall of water would be sent straight up and then hurled by the wind against the windshield and into the back of the boat. Soon we started to wallow.

We tacked west to roll with the waves. This reduced the pounding and improved the wind angle, but our new course would take us far to the south and would nearly double the distance we had to travel.

There was never any question of turning back. John had purchased the boat to handle exactly these conditions or worse. To give in now would be to admit the folly of his purchase. We stopped to bail out and the punishment diminished; but as soon as we started again the waves came at us with renewed ferocity.

When we reached the opposite shore we had to turn back to challenge the waves off our port bow. We made even slower progress on that tack. It seemed like an eternity before we finally limped past Grape Island and into the narrows leading to Lake Couchiching. We were cold and sodden and badly in need of a hot shower. A crossing that should have taken us 30 minutes had taken three times that long.

We tied up at the public dock in Orillia and changed into dry clothing. A quick hot breakfast at a nearby coffee shop and we were on our way again.

The northeast wind continued. Couchiching is about one-tenth the size of Simcoe, and the waves were correspondingly smaller, but we still had to proceed slowly. John's impatience was palpable.

"Er, Gordy, uh, I think we'll head straight for Honey Harbour when we get to the Bay rather than drop you off first at your place in Penetang. Di can drive round to pick you up, okay? Don't want to be late for my guests."

I just looked at John. Some gratitude! He was just trying me on for size. The round trip drive from Penetang to Honey Harbour would probably take Di two and a half hours and he knew it. I held his gaze until he turned away. The prospect of Di's reaction to his suggestion doubtless gave him pause for thought.

It was mid-morning when we negotiated Couchiching Lock and entered the Severn River. From there we would cross Sparrow Lake and continue along 20 miles of wide navigable Severn River Waterway until we reached the marine railway at Big Chute. Then a couple of small hops would take us into Georgian Bay.

ى ى ى

There was still a blustery wind but no sign of rain as we tied up at the dock at Big Chute shortly after noon. Soon we were shunted onto a trolley that raised us on tracks a few feet out of the water and then started down the 57-foot vertical drop to the waters below. Beside us cascaded the waters of the original Big Chute. A sign advised boaters to start their motors briefly once they were out of the water to clear the exhausts.

"No way. We're not running the engine of this boat on dry land, that's for sure," said John with great finality. "Any fool knows that's bad for the pump impellor."

"It's only for a couple of seconds, John, just to clear the water from the exhausts while the boat is still pointed uphill. That way when she tilts downwards, water won't drain back through the exhaust manifolds into the engine."

John acknowledged the wisdom of this advice, but his arguing took too long. We were actually near the bottom of our descent when he fired up the engine, the water in the exhausts having long since backed up. A small crowd was gathered to watch the boats being relaunched. John's timing was perfect. The engine caught just as we started to level out, the angle perfect for maximum crowd dispersal. Our twin exhausts exploded like two fully primed water canon with devastating effect. Amid the general confusion John rushed to the stern proffering a box of Kleenex to members of the drenched assembly. I busied myself in the cabin.

We passed through the narrow confines of Little Chute and into the waters of Gloucester Pool, a picturesque body of water strongly reminiscent of the Muskoka Lakes just to the northeast. Only five miles now separated us from the final lock at Port Severn, entrance to Georgian Bay.

"John, I've been searching everywhere for your Port Severn/Georgian Bay chart. Any idea where it is?"

"Oh, my charts don't go down that far. Never had a need for them. But don't worry, I know the Georgian Bay like the back of my hand."

"But have you ever been to Port Severn by water?"

"No, but I'm sure the channel's well marked."

An icicle stabbed at my ribs. I had often studied the chart of that extreme southeast corner of Georgian Bay with morbid fascination. It was pockmarked with little crosses and warnings of dangerous shoals.

"My God, Frise, do you realize what we're heading into? You want us to run that gauntlet without a chart? Are you crazy?"

But that's just what we had to do. As soon as we left the channel we were lost. Without a chart we couldn't set a course. We scanned the horizon for the Penetang water tower, generally a useful navigation point, but we couldn't even see as far as the shore of Midland Bay. Worse, the grey skies reflected flat on the water, concealing the hungry fangs lurking beneath the surface. All around us waves broke on exposed rocks. We proceeded very slowly, hearts pounding. I concentrated on the greyness ahead. Ghostly shapes took form then dissipated.

Suddenly out of the obscurity an island loomed about half a mile ahead.

"John, that may be Present Island. Give it a wide berth. If it's Present, it's alive with shoals."

We headed further south. We didn't want to go north of Present Island in this poor visibility. We both knew that in the 1940s a passenger boat carrying a hockey team had taken that route, missed the large channel marker off the south end of Beausoleil Island and gone aground. Half of those on board drowned.

As we groped our way forward, the conviction grew on me that something wasn't right. I had often fished around Present Island for pickerel and Northern pike, and this didn't look at all familiar. Nervously we felt our way forward, watchful for any change in the colour of the water that would betray a lurking dragon's maw. All at once the gloom parted to reveal a solid shoreline of trees and houses dead ahead.

I felt a surge of relief. "Hey, John, that's the shore of Midland Bay ahead! We're way too far south. We wound up crossing right over the middle of the Bay"

We followed the shoreline north around Midland Point and headed toward Penetang until at last we could see the familiar water tower. With a great sigh we entered the harbour.

Later, retracing our course on the chart, we could only marvel at how we had contrived to avoid a watery grave. Someone, somewhere, had been looking after the four of us.

ৼ ৼ ৼ

At the sound of our horn a screen door slammed and Di came running down the lawn, preceded by Sophie. Absorbed in the triumph of the moment, two homecoming heroes, I had completely forgotten about Tramp.

But Tramp had not forgotten about Sophie, whose appearance stirred bitter memories. With one great leap he was ashore intent on settling accounts. Sophie made a desperate bid to reach the sanctuary of the cottage but there was no contest. By the time Di reached them, Sophie was pinned to the lawn in a vise-grip, yelping blue murder.

Frise jumped onto the dock and stamped his foot.

"Tramp! Bad dog! Back off!"

But Di already had Tramp by the muzzle and inserted her fingers in his mouth, pressing his upper lip against his teeth. He meekly backed off and Sophie retreated to the cottage, tail between her legs. Tramp ran off in the opposite direction. Frise stood there in awe.

"Welcome home, intrepid travellers," Di smiled, wiping her hand. "Have fun?" She wrinkled her nose. "My, but you two are a bit whiffy."

She turned to give me a welcoming kiss then saw my face.

"Good grief, G.G., what on *earth* have you done to your face? Been in a fight?"

"Only doing my bit for conservation, love," I said, enjoying Frise's discomfiture.

We walked back to the dock and Di stopped dead in her tracks. The Raven was a sorry sight. Her torn top hung askew and her hatch cover still suffered its identity crisis. Inside, the cockpit had all the earmarks of a recent tornado.

"You came all the way in *that?* I mean, you actually *slept* beneath that toilet contraption?"

Frise chuckled, jumped in and started the engine, Tramp hard on his heels.

"Ah, Di, wait till I get her all fixed up. You won't believe how beautiful she'll look. She's a real classic."

"She's a classic, all right," said Di.

"Yes, well, have to go. 'Bye, Di, 'bye, Gordy. See you next week."

He cast off as I pushed them out and he fired up the engine. The growl turned to a snarl, then to a defiant raspberry of marine flatulence as they headed up the harbour and disappeared behind Magazine Island.

7

Inheritance

IN THE FALL of 1973, more than a year after our Trent adventure, John invited me for lunch at the National Club to discuss an "unusual investment opportunity of great importance." He had reserved a table in the south alcove of the main dining room where we would have more privacy.

He looked furtively over his shoulder as we sat down, and thanked me in a subdued voice for joining him. He wasn't fooling me. I was pretty sure this so-called opportunity concerned the Raven. Pre-emptive action was called for.

"Well, John," I said in a normal voice, "what's on your mind? Nothing to do with the Raven, I suppose?"

He looked chagrined.

"Come on, John, it's not hard to figure out. You said you wanted to discuss an unusual investment opportunity. If it had anything to do with business you'd have simply come to my office. This thing had to be something more personal, and what could be more personal than the Raven?"

"Ah Gordy yes. You always were one step ahead of me. See, I've been given the chance to buy this fantastic Norwegian boat, the "Windy 22." You should see her, Gordy, classic lines stem to stern, fast inboard/outboard, built to true yachtsmen's standards."

His hands and arms were doing the talking and I knew all the words by heart.

"I see. And so you want to get rid of the Raven?"

"Why no, of course not, well, that is, I thought I'd give you first opportunity to buy her, you know, seeing as you already recognize her true worth. I'll let you have her for the $1,800 I paid for her, even though I spent that much again fixing her up."

"Let me get this straight. You want to replace the Raven with another 22-foot boat, and you're prepared to leave $1,800 on the table in the process? What's wrong with the Raven?"

"Nothing's wrong with the Raven – er, that is, nothing that you don't know about. She is difficult for Libby to handle, and she doesn't shed the waves properly in a cross wind, and oh well I might as well be up-front with you. Libs has put her foot down. I have to sell the Raven."

"And somehow the Windy will magically solve your problems?"

"Absolutely. She has modern lines with a bow flare, and she handles like a dream. Oh and one other thing . . ."

He leaned over toward me and looked briefly over his shoulder again before disclosing the last grisly detail.

". . . she's fibreglass."

He mumbled the word, half swallowing it like a spoonful of medicine. Then his tongue made its traditional punctuation point and he sat looking at me defiantly, traitor to the cause of all wooden boat owners.

"Fibreglass?" I asked. "Did you say fibreglass? You want to buy a plastic bathtub? Don't you know how she'll pound in a rough sea?"

"I know she'll pound a bit more, but at least she won't ship all that water, either over the side or through the hull."

"Wait a minute. Through the hull? You mean the Raven leaks?"

"Hell no, she's as tight now as she was on our trip. But you know it's only a matter of time with wooden boats."

He was manipulating me, playing on my weakness for wooden boats. He knew that I had reached the outer edges of frustration with the leaky old Hunter and was ripe for the picking.

I prevaricated but it was no use. By the end of lunch I had assumed ownership of the Raven. No haggling, no conditions, cheque signed on the spot. To have and to hold.

᛭ ᛭ ᛭

Di greeted the news of my latest acquisition with predictable enthusiasm.

"You mean you actually paid good money for that rat trap, the one that almost killed the two of you?"

There were now two women in my family, not counting our two and a half-year-old daughter Andy, and the scales were tipped. I feared the worst. Hell hath no fury.

᛭ ᛭ ᛭

Important things were happening to my career at this time. In late 1973 I left Nesbitt Thompson to join Slater Walker, the British merchant bank. This move turned out to be short-lived because a year later the new Foreign Investment Review Act abruptly curtailed Slater Walker's acquisition activities in Canada. So I changed jobs again, this time to join Morgan Stanley, the U.S. investment bank. The latter involved a move to Montreal in early 1975.

My duties at Slater Walker diverted my attention from the Raven who languished the first half of 1974 in dry dock. In late July I finally managed to visit the boat storage where I had left her the previous fall. Pete Stevens claimed to be a specialist in wooden boats but he was really a quack. He had leased the old Breithaupt Tannery premises on Fox Street near our cottage and was trying to scratch a living out of providing winter storage and boat repair services to unsuspecting wooden boat owners.

The Raven lay in the old tannery shed, covered with grime and tilted at an odd angle. One trestle was taking most of the weight on one side, just ahead of the engine, away from any structural support. She looked pathetic, crippled. A puff of wind caught the tannery door and it gave a low, creaking groan.

"Pete, how long has she been in that position?"

"Since we took her out of the water last fall, why?"

"Hell, Pete, that side of the hull's taking all the weight. That could twist the ribs."

"Nah. These boats are built like a brick shithouse. She'll be fine."

"Yes well please clean her up, give the bottom a good scraping and a coat of anti-fouling paint. I'll be back next week."

☙ ☙ ☙

The Raven was hanging in the slings, her floorboards awash.

"How long has she been in the water?"

"Oh, not long – Thursday morning. Took me until then to clean her up and paint the bottom. She needs a while longer to soak up."

"When did you last pump her out?"

"First thing this morning."

I switched on the bilge pump. It was soon apparent where the water was pouring in: on the port side just ahead of the engine – where she had been improperly supported all winter.

"Pete, she's not going to soak up, because you can see where the water's pouring in – right where that trestle was. I'm holding you responsible for this. I want her totally fixed for next weekend."

"No problem. Couple screws should do it."

"Just make sure I have a dry boat for next weekend."

Now I was really concerned. I knew that a leaking lapstrake boat is difficult to fix once the frame has been warped. In boats with edge-to-edge construction you can just tap caulking in between the planks. But with a lapstrake you can't do that because it forces the overlapping planks apart. The leaking can sometimes be stopped temporarily by applying one of various band-aid compounds to the outside of the hull, but the planks work against each other and soon the layers peel away. The only effective way to stop the leaking is to put more screws through the hull and into the ribs to force the planks back against each other and onto the frame. Each time this is done the boat is weakened. Eventually major surgery is required to replace or fortify the damaged planks and ribs.

☙ ☙ ☙

Pete Stevens cockily led me down to a dry Raven floating high against the dock.

"There you are, dry as a bone."

I lifted the floorboards and inspected the area of previous leakage. It looked like the reverse side of a dartboard. At least two dozen sharp screwtips protruded half an inch on the inside, many of them nowhere close to the supporting ribs. It didn't take much imagination to foresee what would happen when the planks started to work. My beautiful companion had been brutally violated.

"Pete you've absolutely riddled her with screws. Look at that, for God's sakes, half of them aren't even into the ribs!"

"Had to do that to stop the leaking. Water kept pouring in, even after I cinched the boards to the ribs."

Unbelievable incompetence, but I had to admit the whole thing was my fault because I simply hadn't checked out the man's credentials. So I smothered my baser instincts and said nothing. I piloted the now dry Raven to her new mooring in front of our cottage and tied her up.

I ran my hand along her gunwales, feeling the trusting warmth of the sun-baked varnish. *Don't worry, old girl, he won't hurt you any more. I'll get you all patched up and restored to your former glory, I promise, then we'll roam together far and wide.*

We understood each other, the Raven and I.

᠀ ᠀ ᠀

On our first shakedown cruise she behaved impeccably. At top speed of 30 knots she turned more readily to starboard than to port, but that was expected; overall I thrilled to her light and responsive touch in both directions. I even managed to replicate the Bensfort Bridge scenario, taught myself to avoid the clash of wills by reducing the revs and swinging the wheel gently to port as soon as the engine started to snarl. The Raven was still trying to prove something, I knew, but I vowed I would eventually get to the bottom of her perverse behaviour and win her trust and respect.

The stub of the summer passed quickly. We made several picnic trips to our favourite islands, took the Raven fishing and water skiing. When she started to leak again I vowed to find appropriate restorative care for the winter months.

A new marina had opened on Fox Street in the former Beatty stove factory, just up the street from the Breithaupt tannery. Bill van Rijn and Casey Spahn were Dutchmen, sailors who knew wooden boats and who had at their disposal the services of an experienced shipwright. They seemed the right sorts, clearly determined to make their new venture a success.

"We'll have to pull the engine to get at the hull," said Bill. "The warping is real bad, but I think we can still salvage the planks. Put a couple of false ribs on the inside to cinch 'em up against. Should last couple years, anyway."

After consulting with the Raven I decided we should cast our lot with them. That winter my companion became one of the first paying guests at the fledgling Dutchman's Cove Marina. This time she was in good hands.

8

Moving On

THE CITY OF WESTMOUNT clings to the side of the mountain close to downtown Montreal, its elegant older houses testament to the fading ascendancy of anglophone Montreal. The house we found, built in 1908 by a British financier, faced south and had a stunning view across the city and over the St. Lawrence River.

We quickly sold the Toronto house, but decided to keep the Penetang cottage as an anchor to windward. Di had family roots there and we both felt strong sentimental ties to the place.

In July the family moved to the cottage and I started the weekly commute from Montreal. I would fly to Toronto on Friday afternoon and rent a car for the one and a half-hour drive, returning early on

Monday morning. I became a human yo-yo. It was a rushed, abbreviated existence.

One evening toward the end of summer Di and I sat on the porch looking down the long-shadowed lawn toward the water. The Raven rocked at her mooring in a pool of gold. We had spent so little time together. I ruefully contemplated the 4:30 A.M. alarm.

"Not much fun, this commuting, is it, Di?" She had borne the brunt of two active fatherless children all week.

"No, Jeedge, this isn't a life. We both love this place, but it's changing. And now we live so far away."

We walked down to the water and turned to look back at the graceful old structure with its jaunty pentagonal tower, winter home to generations of raccoons and other non-paying guests. We had just replaced a large section of the rotting foundation at great cost. I spoke what was on both our minds.

"I think we should sell the cottage, Di."

She nodded slowly.

"It's all changing so," she said. "This used to be such a secluded part of the bay, well beyond the end of the old railway line. Now it's different. I've known it since Grampy's place next door was sold and turned into a hotel, and now there's a trailer park just down the road and the new marinas. It's time to move on."

Maintenance costs, deteriorating environment, distance: three persuasive reasons to follow our instincts. We put the old cottage on the market and it sold a few weeks later to a University of Toronto professor. Included in the package were the old Hunter and a thousand memories. But I kept the Raven. She went into dry dock at Dutchman's Cove Marina.

❧ ❧ ❧

Career-wise, things were going very well for me. I soon began to realize the benefits of belonging to an important international firm. Morgan Stanley Canada's principal activity was raising funds in the U.S. and international capital markets for major Canadian corporations. Since these funds were often available at lower rates than in the domestic market, and few Canadian firms at that time had the expertise to gain ready access to those markets, our services were much in demand. Soon I was spending much of my time on the road, consummating transactions in Toronto and as far away as Calgary and Vancouver.

Weekends became increasingly precious. We rented a farmhouse for the winter in the rolling hills of the Eastern Townships of Quebec, not far from the town of Cowansville. The owner was an absentee landlord who rented the working farm to a local farmer. Friday evenings we would bundle the kids and Sophie into Di's Volvo and make the 90-minute drive along the Eastern Townships Autoroute to the farm.

The barn had a full complement of cows. It was very cold, and the snow squeaked when we took the kids over to watch a milking or to witness a calf birth. Inside the farmhouse kitchen we kept a huge woodburning stove alight night and day, and the room was always warm when we returned from tobogganing. Those weekends brought us all closer together and made us realize that we had to find a summer replacement for Penetang.

One day as spring approached we took out a map and drew a 100-mile radius around Montreal – the maximum distance we thought would be a reasonable commute. The many lakes in the Laurentians to the north looked very attractive but you could see they were closed in by the mountains; the same could be said to a lesser degree for the larger Lakes Memphramagog and Massawippi in the Townships to the east. We wanted wide open spaces and distant horizons, more like Georgian Bay.

We zeroed in on Lake Champlain, directly south of Montreal. The north end of this 90-mile long lake caresses the Canadian border, while the length of it occupies the rift between New York State's Adirondack Mountains to the west and Vermont's Green Mountains to the east. At its Canadian end Lake Champlain is shallow, flat and uninteresting; but farther south the mountains form a spectacular backdrop to the rolling countryside surrounding the lake. We decided to look for a cottage to rent somewhere on the Vermont side.

I discussed our plans with Jim Taylor, a colleague at Morgan Stanley whose family owned a farm near Middlebury, Vermont. Jim spoke glowingly of a summer lakeside community halfway between Burlington and Middlebury. He promised to invite us down to Vermont to meet Peter and Gay Regan, Vermont friends who summered at Thompson's Point.

❧ ❧ ❧

It was a warm, breezy day in May, and the surrounding hills burst with new greenery and birdsong. We had just finished an energetic set of doubles.

"Tell me about Thompson's Point, Peter."

"It's not far from here, actually. Older summer homes built on a point that hooks out onto the lake to make a south-facing bay. Near Charlotte." He pronounced it Chuh-*lot*.

"I don't think I know Charlotte – this is our first visit to this part of Vermont."

"Oh. Well you know where Burlington is of course. Charlotte's about 12 miles south of Burlington, just off Highway 7, right near where the ferry comes in from Essex on the New York side. Thompson's Point is about three miles down the lake from there."

"How many families are there on the Point?"

"Mmmm, not sure – 30, 40, maybe? The cabins are all different and mostly in their original condition – some large, some small, some on the water, some inland. The land is owned in common by the Association. There's a tennis club and a community beach. It's all very rustic and quite special."

"Are most of the residents local Vermonters like yourselves?"

"Heavens no, quite the contrary. They're second, third and even fourth generation owners, spread out all over the continent, from Alaska to California to Texas and even to Canada. They all come back to their favourite watering hole every summer. Very few properties ever change hands."

I was intrigued.

"Any of the properties ever rented?"

"Rarely. A couple of locals occasionally let their places out for the summer, but these are always snapped up. We're very fussy about whom we let in, you know," he winked.

"What about the lake itself? Is there good swimming, fishing?"

"The best. Lovely clear water. We swim every day June through September right in front of our cabin."

"Sounds idyllic. What about the boating?"

"Aaaaah, the boating, yes . . ."

He turned toward the breeze coming off the distant lake and took a deep breath.

"Mmmmmmmm, fabulous, fabulous. Great winds for sailing. Wide open spaces, sparkling water. Lots of interesting places to visit up and down the lake. Season's almost upon us already! Be glad to take you out if you're in the vicinity. Why do you ask?"

"Oh, it's just that we have this old boat in Ontario and we –"

"You own a boat? What kind, a sailboat?"

"No, a wooden power boat."

"A wooden boat?" Peter was all attention now. "How big is she? What make?"

"22-footer made by Century."

"Ah – '*Century, Thoroughbred of Boats.*' Know them well. What model?"

"A Raven."

"A *Raven?* You actually own a Century *Raven?* This is fantastic. My good friend Wally's going to go ballistic. Another Raven on the lake? It's too good to be true.

"But we don't even have a place . . ."

"Hey, Gay," he called across the court ignoring my protest, "you won't believe this. The Greens have a Century Raven, the same boat that Wally has. You know, the one that's sinking all the time?"

Out of the corner of my eye I saw Di raise her eyes heavenward. Peter enthusiastically pumped my hand.

"Any person who owns a Century Raven is a friend of mine," he announced. "This is incredible news. I'm going to put out enquiries. I'm sure we'll find you a place at Thompson's Point somehow."

⚓ ⚓ ⚓

Peter called the following Monday.

"I've found just the place for you. Nice property, waterfront, facing west across the lake. Professor from Middlebury College, one of the locals I told you about. He's going away on a year's sabbatical next month and wants to rent the property for the entire summer."

He gave me the owner's name and phone number.

9

The Rangoon Country Club

WE DROVE SOUTH through the town of St.-Jean-Sur-Richelieu and soon left the Richelieu River behind and headed cross country toward the border town of Philipsburg. On the road before us and on all sides unfolded mile after mile of drabness, relieved by rundown farmhouses, rusting machinery and the occasional small church adorned with aluminum paint.

The scenery changed abruptly just after Philipsburg. As we emerged from U.S. customs and joined Route 89 south, the foothills of the Green Mountains came down to greet us in a riot and the country was verdant and beautiful. We concluded that the border's abrupt change was no freak accident but part of a Grand Design, penance for French and British transgressions at Fort Ticonderoga two centuries earlier.

We drove a divided and uncrowded highway whose north and south bound lanes wandered their separate ways among the hills. Just past Burlington we exited south along rural Highway 7. This took us through Shelburne and on to the Charlotte turnoff.

The winding country road from Charlotte to Thompson's Point yielded gracefully to our impatience. It sang of the beauties of rural Vermont, leading us through fields and copses alive with the breath of spring, showing us prosperous farms, harbingers of an abundance of local produce.

No formal entry portal marked Thompson's Point, but it was hard to mistake the place. Attractive clapboard houses peeped discreetly through the trees on both sides of the road. They sat atop bluffs and hillocks, on the level ground by the road, down by the waterfront. Most were painted white or in soft pastel shades. They had old-fashioned verandahs and wooden screen doors; many were still boarded up for the season.

"Well, here we are," said Di, navigating. "The directions say to continue straight to the tennis courts."

The quaint old clubhouse with pagoda-like roof presided over the clay courts, its spacious verandah replete with rocking chairs and settees.

"Oh, neat," Di clapped her hands, "the Rangoon Country Club." The name stuck.

I parked the car and walked over to the court. A man in whites was just finishing brushing the immaculate clay surface with a heavy broom.

"Morning."

He looked up and smiled. "Oh, hi, didn't hear you come up. Can I help?"

"Are we on the right road to the Sillcox house?"

"Ah, the new tenants," he said, "I'm Paul Godfrey."

"And I'm Gordon Green, and that's Diana in the car." He waved and we shook hands. "Actually we're not tenants, at least not yet. Simon suggested we come over and take a look at the place."

He laughed. "You won't be disappointed. Just follow the road a couple hundred yards, then walk up the hill to your right. Large yellow house, last one, can't miss it. You need help, just holler – we'll be here most of the morning."

The cottage reminded us of Penetang, spacious and similar in style but lacking the latter's graceful architecture. It stood at the top of a 50-foot bluff overlooking the lake. Between cottage and cliff was a band of dense cedar shrubbery. The taller cedars had been topped to preserve the view.

We stood on the verandah and looked across at the New York side. The lake was quite narrow at this point – only about three miles across – and it seemed we could reach out and touch the far shore where the lush green foothills began their upward scramble toward the mountains. The Adirondacks formed a magnificent backdrop of seven diminishing layers of blues and purples, their crests sharp against the sky as in a Japanese screen. We could only imagine what the sunsets must be like.

The bluff's edge led to a sharp promontory at the north end. There a gazebo had been built facing up the lake toward Canada. We sat in the gazebo and watched the little ferry making its way across to Essex Landing, little realizing how many countless hours we would spend at that same spot, scanning the horizon for a distant black speck.

"This is really special," I said. "Spose we should look inside."

"Oh, Jeedge, I don't care, I love it. As long as the cottage works I think we should take it. I can't imagine anything bad enough to make us want to look any further. Let's just move in right away!" She gave me a hug.

The house was spacious, clean and well furnished. If either of us had any lingering doubts, they evaporated with the brief house tour.

On our way back we detoured along the bluff in the other direction and found a pathway through the cedar shrubbery to the face of the cliff. Here crude steps, hewn out of the loose shale, led down to the beach. A rope handrail, fastened to old roots and the occasional spike driven into the shale, followed the precarious stairway down.

I tested the rope and it held, so I went down. Near the top, the steps were few and far between and I had to turn to face the rock and feel with my foot for the next step. Otherwise, it was like walking down a steep staircase.

"Come on down, Di," I called up, "it's quite safe." I climbed up to help her get started. Once she was over the tricky part she gained in confidence, and soon we were both standing at the bottom.

A large slab of broken cliff presided over our beach and created a sheltered suntrap. Wild purple iris and creeping phlox blossomed among the fissures in the shale, and butterflies spread trembling wings on the rocky faces. Truck-sized pieces of shale, some half in the water and some totally submerged, formed natural swimming ledges to the depths beyond. The water was clear and inviting even this early in the season. It was totally private: no one could possibly see us from above, and access along the beach was difficult.

We got back into the car in high spirits and tooted the horn at Paul as we drove by the tennis courts. If that made him lose the next point, we never heard about it.

ৡ ৡ ৡ

Thompson's Point welcomed us in early July. I took my vacation at the start of our rental and soon we were part of that friendly community. We frequently played tennis with the Regans and Peter would ask me about the Raven.

"Well, Cap'n Green, is that legendary craft of yours ever going to make an appearance? I've told Wally all about it, and his Raven's so hot and bothered it can't stop leaking, ha-ha."

In truth I was undecided what to do about the Raven. I never realized how much I would miss her. I tried to analyze my *grande passion* and concluded that it was more than simple infatuation on my part. It was the contrast of her headstrong behaviour and her pathetic vulnerability that somehow filled a deep and unsuspected void left by an unhappy part of my childhood. I needed her, and she needed me, and that's how it was. And now I had abandoned her. The thought of her sitting in the sheds at Dutchman's Cove, patiently awaiting my return, near drove me to distraction. The more I thought about her, the more I was determined to bring her from Georgian Bay to Lake Champlain.

My first impulse was to bring her all the way by water. This would involve retracing our steps to Rice Lake along the Trent Waterway, then continuing on to Lake Ontario, down the St. Lawrence Seaway past Montreal to Sorel, and finally up the Richelieu River to Lake Champlain – a total distance of nearly 700 miles. The problem was that I simply couldn't afford the time to do this myself – and besides, Di mistrusted her rival too much to agree to such an outrageous plan, even though she would be along as chaperone.

So we discussed other ways of bringing her out. One idea I had was to make a father-son bonding trip with ten-year-old Doug the following spring. This scheme was scarcely more realistic than taking Di along, but the idea was appealing enough that I put off making any other concrete arrangements.

Still, I yearned for the day when I could hear once more her irascible snarl, feel her pulsing urgency beneath my fingertips, the wind in my hair.

ৡ ৡ ৡ

Vacation over, I reverted to commuting on weekends. It was a busy time at the office. One transaction that took a lot of my time was a debenture financing for a British Columbia forest products company. That deal entailed making several trips to Vancouver, accompanied by Jim Fletcher, a young Associate whom we had hired out of the Harvard Business School that spring.

Jim was bright and articulate, filled with boyish enthusiasm and humour. An Engineering graduate from Queen's University, he had spent a couple of years with Allan Crawford Associates, a manufacturer's representative for precision electronic equipment, before enrolling for graduate studies at Harvard. His numbers skills and his ability to sell his ideas coherently and logically made him an excellent candidate for investment banking.

On the flights to and from Vancouver we got to know each other better. Jim had grown up in the Eastern Townships of Quebec and his family summered in North Hatley on Lake Massawippi where he did a fair amount of boating.

In his two years at Allan Crawford's firm, Jim and Paul Spafford, another engineering graduate (University of Waterloo) who now worked for competitor Wood Gundy, had criss-crossed the country in an elaborately equipped company van selling sophisticated electronic test equipment to universities, hospitals and research facilities. Jim's entertaining account of the escapades of those two footloose bachelors took most of a flight back from Vancouver in the telling. Their carefree, swashbuckling approach to life should have put me on Red Alert, but it didn't.

Inevitably I came to telling Jim about the Raven and my frustrated dream of bringing her to Lake Champlain.

"By water all the way from Georgian Bay, you say? Hey, that sounds like fun. I could do that for you!"

An angel trilled somewhere up there in the firmament. I slowly reached for my glass.

"Uh, Jim, that's quite a trip. I'm not sure you quite underst . . ."

"No, no, seriously, I do understand, it's a fabulous idea. I'd love to do it. Paul would just go nuts. We're both keen boaters. If you really want that boat brought over to Lake Champlain next summer, we're the perfect team. I'll check with him in the morning and let you know."

And suddenly there was with the angel a multitude of the heavenly host, belting out the *Halleluiah Chorus*. I signalled ecstatically for another drink.

10

Paul and Hiawatha, Jim and Tippyssing

SATURDAY, JULY 2, 1977, foot of the town dock in Penetanguishene. It was still early morning, but Paul was already there, his car parked on the dock beside the Raven. He stood talking to Bill van Rijn.

"Morning, Bill, morning, Paul," I said.

"Morning, fellas," said Paul, ostentatiously consulting his watch. "Good of you to come. We're all loaded up and ready to go, thanks to Bill here."

Jim and I had stayed in Toronto most of the week, working on a Euro debt financing for Hudson's Bay Company that we had finally put to bed the previous evening. We had left our hotel early that morning. Paul had flown in from Montreal a day ahead to purchase the provisions.

The Raven had been de-winterized and launched the week before. Bill had suggested we rendezvous at the public dock instead of Dutchman's Cove Marina so we could drive right out to the boat and load her from there. The wisdom of that advice was now evident.

"Any leaking problems, Bill?" I asked, eyeing the Raven who seemed low in the water.

"Not too bad, considering. Remember she's been out of the water two seasons. I tightened her up best I could. She's quite dry right now."

"She is?"

I looked dubiously at the Raven who seemed to settle even lower in the water. Only then did I focus on her cargo.

She was loaded for a safari through Darkest Africa. Khaki tents, tarpaulins, duffel bags, stove, and heavy duty raingear were piled to the gunwales. A pair of army boots hung from the gearshift. Large water containers and cases of canned beans and Spam were jammed on each side of the engine box. Sitting on top of the engine box was this large reinforced steel chest.

"Good grief, Paul, she looks like the African Queen. What on earth's in that monstrous chest?"

Paul jumped on board and heaved up the lid.

"Ta-daaa!"

It was an army surplus ice chest filled with ice blocks and Molson Export. Squirrelled away in one corner were a couple of pints of milk and a package of butter.

"I see you'll not be wanting for liquid sustenance," said Bill. "No wonder that chest was so heavy. I don't imagine the contents could ever impair your navigational prowess."

I was thinking the same thing, as evidently was the Raven, for a strangled gurgle issued from her exhausts.

"Well, ha-ha, of course not," said Paul, vigorously rubbing his hands. "Anyway, we should get a move on – lots of territory to cover. Throw your stuff on board, Fletch – no, not on the ice box please. Any special instructions, Gordon?"

The poor Raven was nearly suffocating under her outrageous burden and these two pirates were oblivious to her discomfort.

"Nothing in particular, Paul, but please go easy on the old girl as she's not as young as she used to be."

"Promise we'll treat her with kid gloves."

"Good! Well you know she's really quite special to me, the old Raven. She's not just any old boat."

Paul started to protest but I had made my point. Time to send them on their way.

"Well what are you guys waiting for? Got the charts?"

"Yup."

"Get the first one out and I'll point you in the right direction."

He spread the chart on top of the ice chest. I oriented it roughly and traced out the route to Port Severn with my finger. Then stepped back and pointed up the bay.

"Head straight north up the harbour. Leave the marker off Magazine Island well to starboard. At the entrance to the harbour you'll pass Champlain's Cross which marks his visit in the 1630s. There you'll turn east, and then you're on your way to Port Severn. Your course will take you not too far from Carhaguha, near Sainte Marie, where Champlain celebrated the first Mass in Ontario on that same visit. And of course your final destination will be Lake Champlain, named after the great explorer himself."

I paused to let the historical significance of this sink in. I liked the symmetry of it all, starting and ending with Champlain. I hoped some of my enthusiasm would rub off on the youthful adventurers.

"Huh," said Fletcher. "Bet Champlain didn't have any Molson Ex."

That set the tone. Bill and I pushed the boat out from the dock, Fletcher at the helm.

"Remember to stop regularly to pump her out," I called out, "she's bound to leak the first couple days. Oh and Jim, listen. That bit about turning to port. If she starts to fight you, for God's sakes remember to throttle her back."

Jim gave a little wave – yeah, Mom, yeah. He opened the throttle and the Raven gave her familiar snarl. Then a certain urgency crept into the cadence as she pulled away, a pulsing, pleading note. I almost ran after her.

꙳ ꙳ ꙳

On the drive back to the airport I was consumed with guilt. I had abandoned her again, this time into the hands of a pair of brutish adventurers. But then, I rationalized, Jim and Paul were professional engineers, both holding responsible positions in their respective firms and both experienced boaters. If I had to commit my precious charge into others' hands, who better qualified? Still I struggled with conflicting emotions. I desperately wanted to be with them, yet I was relieved I wouldn't have to endure the indignities that surely awaited them, for I knew the Raven would not take her abandonment lightly. Heaven only knew what pranks she would get up to, what revenge she might wreak.

After landing in Montreal I drove straight down to Vermont where Di was already ensconced with the family. The kids came running down the hill and assaulted me as I climbed out of the car. After clowning around a bit, I gave Doug my overnight bag and piggybacked Andy up to the house where Di greeted me with a hug.

"How'd it go, Hon?" she asked.

"Fine."

"Your black mistress still in one piece?"

"Just. She's leaking worse, and she's laden to the gills, I mean really laden. You wouldn't believe what they've piled into her. Enough beer and provisions to last a year, mostly beer!"

"But you met up okay?"

"Yup, right on schedule and they're well on their way now. But funny thing, Di, that boat's almost human. I swear she . . . anyway I can't help worrying. I know Jim and Paul are big boys and experienced boaters, both of them engineers. But I'll sure feel better when they phone tonight."

But there was no phone call that evening, nor on Sunday either. Early Monday morning I drove to Montreal and went straight to the office. No message there. I couldn't concentrate on my work. Surely they would call just to let me know they were all right?

By the time I got home that evening I was frantic. I phoned Di again in Vermont to check they hadn't called. I moped around the empty house, finally decided I'd give them one more day. If I hadn't heard by the end of Tuesday I would notify the Coast Guard.

I didn't have to wait that long. A telex was waiting at the office Tuesday morning, sent the previous evening and rife with the political insensitivities of the era:

DEAR GORDON

STRUCK ROCKS AT MILE 13. FOUND FRIENDLY INDIAN RESERVE AND TRADED BOTH HALVES OF BOAT FOR ONE MORE CANOE TWO SQUAWS AND THREE [CASES] OF MOLSON . . . IN OUR JUDGEMENT TRADE WAS IN EXCESS OF FAIR MARKET VALUE. E.T.A. NOW EXPECTED TO BE ONE FORTNIGHT AND A CHANGE OF THE

MOON. BREWERS RETAIL REFUSE CHARGEX AND
WAMPUM. PLEASE WIRE FUNDS TO GENERAL
POST OFFICE PETERBORO TO ARRIVE NO LATER
THAN JULY 20. WILL PHONE IF ANY SOCIAL
PROBLEMS CROP UP.
LOVE,

PAUL AND HIAWATHA
JIM AND TYPISSING

Anxiety dissipated into relief which exploded into joyful mirth. My
spirits took wing. I rushed into Jim Taylor's office and plonked the telex
on his desk. He let out a howl and soon most the office was gathered
round Jim's desk loudly guffawing and backslapping. Quite unseemly
behaviour against the dignified decorum usually observed in Morgan
Stanley's elegant offices. But then all had been party to my growing
angst.

Marie-France the receptionist stuck her head around the corner.
"Phone call for you, Monsieur Green."

I ran through to my office. The call was collect from Fletcher.

"Fletch! Just got your telex. Paul and Hiawatha! What a couple of
idiots! Seriously I was getting worried. Is everything okay? How's the
Raven?"

He cleared his throat.

"Well, Gordon, a bit of a setback . . ."

Uh-oh.

"We hit a reef going through Hell's Gate on Stony Lake."

Jesus.

"You mean your telex was serious?"

"More like ESP. As we were leaving the post office where we sent the
telex this guy in a ski boat offered to show us a shortcut through to the
main channel. Said he knew the lake like the back of his hand. It was
getting late so we took him up on his offer. He was pulling a skier, never
looked back to check on us, and we didn't even bother to look at the
chart. Whammo! Prop hit a rock at full speed."

"Oh my God." The impact punched me in the stomach. "How much
damage is there, Jim?"

"Well, the prop's a goner for sure, and the shaft's badly bent. She's
now in Bayview Marina in Burleigh. They've ordered a new prop and
sent the shaft away to be straightened and machined. Hope to have her
back together in three, four days. No other damage far as we can tell."

"What will you do now?"

"Just hang around, I guess."

I counted to ten.

"Okay, Jim, well listen, don't worry about this. I'll speak to my insurance agent about the cost of repair – I'm sure we're fully covered other than the deductible. I'm just relieved the hull wasn't damaged."

"So are we, believe you me. But that's pretty decent of you, Gordon. I'm really sorry. You can reach us through the marina – we'll stick close by. And we'll keep you posted on progress."

"Jim – one question before you go."

"Yeah?"

"How come it took you so long to reach Stony Lake?"

"Uh, well, long story, Gordon. Slight navigational problems. Couldn't find Port Severn. Spent the first day wandering around Georgian Bay."

Again that icicle in my ribs. Vision of hungry fangs lurking beneath the pock-marked surface of that treacherous corner of the Bay. Another miraculous delivery, perhaps, but not an auspicious beginning.

꙳ ꙳ ꙳

John Fuller, my insurance agent, rounded out my day.

"Gordon, you're not going to like this."

That persistent icicle.

"You let the insurance lapse when you sold the cottage, remember? The boat was part of a package policy. Afraid you're simply not covered."

The earth rocked beneath my feet. Sharp shards of ice caressed my liver.

"John," I pleaded desperately, "surely there's something we can do. I mean, what about my homeowner's policy?"

"Doesn't extend to boats. You'll just have to chalk it up to experience."

"Well you'd better insure her now, John."

"Done, as of this minute. Same coverage as before?"

"Yes. Grrrrr."

꙳ ꙳ ꙳

I phoned Jim at the marina, offered to split the cost of repairs fifty-fifty as the lack of insurance was my fault.

"That seems more than fair, Gordon, we appreciate that. But don't worry about us. We'll be fine. Three or four days and we'll be on our way again."

"It's not you I'm worried about, just my boat. Please don't hit any more reefs or my insurance rates will go up." Big joke.

On Saturday Jim called me down in Vermont to say that the prop and shaft had arrived and hopefully the boat would be ready first thing Monday. A girl's laughter rippled in the background. More laughter and the clink of glasses. Evidently their enforced idleness in Stony Lake vacationland was not all hardship. *Why weren't they outside, minding the Raven?*

꙳ ꙳ ꙳

The next call came Wednesday afternoon.

"We're well on our way, Gordon. Left Monday afternoon and making good time."

"No more mishaps?"

"Nothing major. Dropped the chrome gas cap overboard this morning. Stuck an old rag in the hole – not elegant, but serves the purpose."

I felt a rush of pity and resentment. The indignities being inflicted on my beautiful companion by these boorish, insensitive oafs!

"I'll order a new gas cap. Where are you now?"

"Near Trenton, heading out to Lake Ontario and the Thousand Islands. Should reach Montreal late Friday."

"Let's see," I said, excitement stirring, "that should get you to Lake Champlain some time Sunday . . ."

"Yeah, but don't forget we have to clear the Seaway locks with all that seagoing traffic. We could reach Sorel by Saturday afternoon, and that would bring us out onto Lake Champlain on Sunday okay. But there may be delays, you know, so don't count on it."

"Okay but at least we know you're getting close, Jim. I'm taking two weeks' vacation and can't wait for you to arrive. We'll keep the champagne on ice."

"Right. Well cheers, Gordon. Better be on our way. Holding up the lock traffic."

"See you Sunday."

For the first time since the saga began I started to believe in the Raven's arrival. My spirits soared at the prospect. We would give her a royal welcome! I should have said break a leg or touch wood or something, but I was feeling confident and excited. Then when Jim called Friday afternoon to say they were at the Seaway locks and right on schedule, the thrill of anticipation was palpable. It was only after he hung up I began to have doubts – small, nagging flutterings.

11

Beached in St.-Jean-Sur-Richelieu

SATURDAY at Thompson's Point was a frenzy of activity. We needed a mooring, somewhere to keep the boat. And a means of getting to and fro. I took Doug to the local sporting goods and marine supply store where we bought a yellow inflatable dinghy, a mooring buoy, a length of chain, a 20-foot pre-spliced mooring line, and some shackles.

A space had to be cleared at the edge of the community beach where we would leave the inflatable. The whole family pitched in to do that, and then we held a formal christening, ginger ale and all. We called the dinghy Yelloweez after Eloise, our new puppy; wrote the name in big black letters on each side with a marker pen. Then I donned mask, snorkel and flippers and set out to find a suitable mooring anchor for the Raven.

The south-facing bay of the community beach slopes gently away from the shore, sand giving way to flat bedrock at a depth of about 15 feet. I wanted to moor the Raven in at least 15 feet of water, close by several other boats already out there. A conventional sand or mud anchor won't hold on bedrock, so I needed a heavy object to take its place. I hoped that I might find such an object already in place, left behind by some previous boater.

No such luck, but I did find a piece of bedrock jutting up from the surrounding flat shale slightly farther out, about 18 feet down. I dove down to inspect this formation and found that the millenia had fashioned it into a perfect anvil with a neat hole in its centre, all still massively part of the bedrock. It seemed an ideal anchor.

I put on my weight belt to give neutral buoyancy and dove down to prepare the anchor. I passed the chain twice around the anvil and then through the hole, resurfacing frequently before I managed to secure it with a shackle. Several dives later I had tightened the locking screw with a pair of pliers and secured it with stainless wire.

I was exhausted. I dove down to retrieve the free end of the chain and found that it was now far too short. I had used most of it to wind around the anvil. Of the original 30 feet only about ten feet remained, about one-third of the length required for adequate scope. So I used the new 5/8-inch mooring line instead. The Raven's own eight-foot bowline was then used as the line from mooring to boat.

I swam ashore and admired my handiwork. The Raven would ride in 18 feet of water at the end of 38 feet – about the recommended 2:1 scope ratio. More important, the mooring was anchored to solid bedrock. Let the south wind blow: there was no way in the world the boat would ever break away from such a solid anchorage – not in my lifetime, anyway.

⚓ ⚓ ⚓

I dreamed the Raven was boarded by gangsters on the St. Lawrence Seaway. They took her to the wharves at Ile Notre Dame where they set her up as a floating unit to display contraband medical diagnostic equipment. A group of white-coated hospital representatives watched a demonstration of the equipment. Jim and Paul struggled bound and gagged in the cuddy cabin up forward.

I awoke with a start. What was that all about? I remembered the dream as clearly as if it were reality. My resentment at the callousness of youth must be boiling near the surface. Or was the Raven subliminally including me in her own dreams?

It was early morning so I slipped down to the ledges. The water was clear and invigorating. I dried myself off and climbed onto one of the large boulders at the foot of the cliff and looked toward the Canadian border. The lake was still asleep. Small wisps of mist hung over the unruffled water. No movement disturbed the tranquil scene. I took a deep breath.

I kept myself occupied most of the morning. Put the champagne in the refrigerator and glasses in the freezer, rechecked the mooring, took the Yelloweez out on a shake-down cruise with the kids. At noon I poured Bloody Marys for Di and myself and went down to the gazebo, scanning the horizon hopefully with my binoculars. Nothing.

I gulped down lunch and returned to the gazebo. Panning across the New York side I picked out a small black dot on the horizon. The Raven! I tracked it for five minutes, excitement growing, then saw a puff of smoke and a tiny funnel amidships. It was a much larger boat, a tug of some sort.

I went back to the gazebo every half hour, searching the lake from right to left, left to right. Every new vessel now looked like the Raven. By cocktail hour Di was ready to have me committed.

"Jeedge, stop pacing up and down like an expectant father. For goodness sakes relax. Your baby will come when it's good and ready."

The phone rang.

"Gordon, it's Jim. I have some very bad news, I'm afraid."

No icicles this time, just a red hot iron spike.

"How bad is bad, Jim?"

"Really bad. We ran the boat up on the sharp rock banks of the Chambly Canal. She very nearly sank as we pulled her off, but the St.-Jean fire department kept her afloat long enough to beach her. That's where we are right now – beached in St.-Jean-Sur-Richelieu."

"My God, Jim, are you both okay? When did this all happen?"

"Couple hours ago. We're both fine. I needed to take a leak, handed the helm over to Paul. We came to a left hand curve in the canal. Paul accelerated to get ahead of the boats who were following closely so I could do my thing over the side, you know ... That's when she suddenly lurched to starboard, just like you said ..."

"Oh good Lord."

"Paul didn't have a chance. He turned hard to the left but she headed straight up onto the rocks. Dreadful crunch."

I felt a wrench, could hear the Raven's pleading note.

"What then?"

"Large cruiser pulled us off. Some kindness! That's when we started to sink. Someone called the fire department, and the noble Pompiers de St.-Jean came within minutes. Drove along the tow path and saved us. Even had a reporter from the local paper at the scene."

"What will you do now?"

"She's being put on a trailer as we speak. They're taking her to the local marina where she'll be safe overnight. We'll take a taxi to my place in Montreal and drive back in the morning. Can you meet us at the marina?"

I sighed.

"See you in the morning."

⚓ ⚓ ⚓

A black cloud hung in the sky as I headed across the flat farmland toward St.-Jean-Sur-Richelieu. I had known with certainty that something like this would happen, that the Raven would be sure to exact further revenge for her abandonment and callous treatment. But I had begun to hope against hope that the worst was behind us. Now I ruefully contemplated another boatless summer.

Fletcher and Spafford awaited me at the marina. Neither looked me in the eye.

"Gordon, I can't tell you how badly we feel about this." Jim forlornly traced patterns in the gravel.

"Fletch, Paul, listen. Sure you were careless. But this is *not* entirely your fault. The boat has serious steering problems. This damage can be repaired. We even have insurance to pay for it. So let's just get on with fixing her, and drop those hang-dog expressions!"

They smiled wanly. The Raven looked pathetic. A jagged hole was pierced into her starboard bow right at the water line. Every few seconds a tear welled up and trickled from the gaping wound to the ground below.

Emil Laurin, the only person in town in any way qualified to repair wooden boats, came by to assess the damage. He inspected the point of impact inside and out, clucking and whistling and sucking through his teeth.

"'E can be repaired, m'sieur, but damage his bad. I need to rebuil' from hinside, you understan'? Will take tree, maybe four week."

"How much will all this cost?"

Again the sucking sound.

"Ah, m'sieur. I need to work hout. Good hoak for keel an' rib, mahogany for 'ull expensive, no?"

"Tell you what. I'll put my insurance agent directly in touch with you. We want the work done as soon as possible. Can you start right away?"

"One other small job she nearly finish. Could start next week."

"No sooner than that?"

"M'sieur, I cannot –"

"Okay, but no later than next week, please? And only the very best workmanship. No short cuts."

"Monsieur."

I had offended the poor man. Canadian unity problems in a microcosm. I did my best to make amends.

"Eh bien, Monsieur Laurin!" I said cheerfully, "Je confie mon bâteau-ci à vos soins. Mon agent d'assurance vous téléfonera tout de suite. Soyez gentil, je vous implore!"

He brightened and talked rapidly for several minutes. I got the gist of what he said and came away with the impression that the Raven was in reasonably competent hands – not that we had much choice.

John Fuller was less enthusiastic.

"They hit *what*? *Who* did you say was driving, the same two id . . . What? Of course you're covered, Gordon. No, it doesn't make any difference who was driving, I was just wondering why on earth you would . . . oh, never mind, I'll call M. Laurin this afternoon and arrange for an adjuster to go out there and look at the boat. No, you don't need to worry about anything else. We'll take everything from here."

᪥ ᪥ ᪥

Fletcher and Spafford had by now used up their allotted vacation time. Nevertheless they insisted on completing their assignment, right down to delivery at Thompson's Point.

"We'll just have to play it by ear, Gordon. We'll try to keep our weekends open."

In late August M.Laurin called to say the Raven was ready. Jim and Paul were both free that weekend. As I drove down to Vermont Friday evening I thought back over the obstacle course they had negotiated that summer. Now at last the saga seemed to be coming to an end. Although the boating season was nearly over, I was excited at the thought of spending a few precious weekends with the Raven before she was retired for the winter.

On my morning visit to the swimming ledges I consciously avoided glancing up the lake. I scrambled back up to the cottage, put the coffee on, and was on my way to the bathroom when the phone rang.

"Gordon, it's Jim. We're at the marina, got here in good time. More delays, I'm afraid. The hull repairs are fine and she's not leaking, but she shakes like a bowl of jelly. Our friends here forgot to re-align the motor once they had the pieces all back together. Say they can't do anything about it till Monday. Better save the champagne for next weekend."

That week the weather broke. After several hot and sultry days a cold front moved through the area and brought with it a series of violent thunderstorms. Lake Champlain is notorious among sailors for its storms. One has only to look at a topographical map to understand the reason: high mountains on either side of the lake converge toward its narrow south end, forming a natural funnel. The wind velocities there in a storm can be extreme.

The storms climaxed toward the end of the week. Saturday was an inside day. Rain pelted the windows as untamed gusts shook loosenesses in the shutters and eaves. The lake was a boiling cauldron of white-flecked, molten lead.

"Good thing the boys aren't out there trying to bring the boat down today," said Di.

"You can say that again – they'd never make it. But the front's supposed to move through this evening. Tomorrow should be sunny and cooler, but quite windy still, from the southeast."

"Wish it was from the north, for their sakes."

"I know."

❦ ❦ ❦

Sunday morning I slept in. The storm dispelled any thought of an early morning swim. I got up and made some tea, fed the kids and got them going, then went back and got into bed with Di and the Sunday *New York Times*. She treasured this one morning of the week she didn't have to be up with the kids.

"Wind doesn't sound quite as strong," she said.

I looked out over the lake.

"Still pretty rough out there, but southeast. We're more sheltered here than in yesterday's north wind. But I'd be happier if it died down some."

The wind dropped during the day. By mid-afternoon, when I started watching for the Raven, it was no more than a fresh breeze with modest whitecaps. The clouds had mostly disappeared and there would be a beautiful sunset.

I was determined not to go through the expectant father routine again. I sauntered down to the gazebo and casually panned the horizon. Several boats pounded their way across the still choppy waters, none resembling the Raven. I walked back to the house whistling.

I busied myself with household chores. Prepared the marinade for the steaks we would share with Jim and Paul. Set up the barbecue, checked the champagne. Looked at my watch: 20 minutes. Swept the verandahs and re-fastened the hammock mountings. Thirty minutes.

My whistle became more strained. By the fourth visit my lips wouldn't quite make the right shape. I kept waiting for the dreaded phone.

Di was feeling the tension too, as were the kids. We all went down to the gazebo. The old structure swayed as the kids ran up and down its steps. I handed watchmaster duties over to Doug.

"Dad, there's something really funny out there."

"Where?"

I took the binoculars.

"There, to the right of Schooner Island. Looks like a submarine with two towers or something."

I focused on where Doug was pointing. A two-humped monstrosity was making its way slowly toward us. We watched it for about five minutes, handing the binoculars back and forth. I had heard rumours of a Lake Champlain Monster . . .

"Dad," cried Doug in great excitement, "it's a boat pulling another boat, that's what it is!"

I looked again. Doug was right. The two towers were two boats attached by a heavy line – the Raven under tow!

Slowly and laboriously the ungainly ensemble made its way toward us. The Raven was being towed by a small outboard and kept pulling one way and then the other, errant thoroughbred shying from its determined handler.

After an hour they were close by the cliffs and within hailing distance.

"Ahoy there, Raven!"

They shouted something I couldn't hear.

I motioned vigorously down the lake.

"Round the point. The mooring's in the bay just around the corner. Meet you there in the dinghy."

They waved acknowledgement.

I ran down to the beach and launched the Yelloweez. Half of
Thompson's Point turned out to witness the grand arrival. As the
comical duo rounded the point the Raven was still straining at right
angles, trying to continue down the lake. Paul grappled the mooring.

"Now what?" I shouted. "Blow a head gasket?"

"Out of gas!"

I rolled my eyes heavenward, half in supplication and half in relief, as
I rowed out to meet them. As I got close enough to reach out and grab
the side, the Raven swung around and pointed her stern directly at me.
There was no question it was deliberate, for the wind had died
completely. She swung, just like that. When I corrected course to pull
alongside, she swung again. Three times I tried to board, and three
times I was presented with her insolent rump. Jim finally reached over
and grabbed the side of the Yelloweez. I wondered why he wasn't
laughing. I felt the eyes of the assembled multitude.

"What a relief," I chuckled nervously as I climbed aboard. "Out of
gas, you say. You two characters are something else. You set off across
Lake Champlain and you run out of gas! Some day I'll have to write a
book about this. No one will ever believe it!"

They said nothing. I had anticipated camaraderie and back-slapping,
but instead there was this flat silence.

"What is it, Jim? There's something wrong, isn't there? There's
something you're not telling me."

"Well," said Paul. "I was driving, and –"

"No, Paul, let me tell it. This isn't going to be easy."

"Okay, Jim," I said, "shoot."

"We made it all the way down the Richelieu River into Lake
Champlain no problem. The boat was running smooth as silk, better
than ever before. No leaking at all.

"Finally we came to the wide open lake. Quite a chop from the
southeast! But we found the Raven could handle it fine as long as we
faced straight into it. So we drew a bead on where we thought
Thompson's Point was and headed straight out. That's when it
happened."

"That's when what happened?"

"That's when we hit the reef."

"Jesus Christ, man!" I exploded. "You hit a reef *again?*"

Dead silence.

"Jim, did you say you hit a reef? What reef? Where was it?"

"It's called Pointe-au-Fer Reef. Right in the middle of the open lake."

"I know Pointe-au-Fer's in the middle. Everybody knows Pointe-au-Fer's in the middle. It's well marked. Didn't you see it on the chart?"

"To be honest we'd put the chart away to keep it dry. Thought we didn't need it now we were on the wide open water. Obviously a serious error."

They both looked absolutely miserable. Slowly I regained my self-control.

"What will I call this chapter in my book?" I muttered under my breath.

"What?"

"Nothing. I was wondering how much damage there was."

"Pretty bad. Probably about the same as Stony Lake. Prop hit with a big crunch, but it's still in one piece because we ran her, very slow and wobbly, all the way down the lake. All the way, that is, until we ran out of gas near Burlington."

"Jesus. What happened then?"

"This guy in the outboard came to our rescue. Went beyond the call of duty. Raven's a brute to tow in choppy waters. He broke all his lines as well as most of the Raven's."

This comedy of errors seemed endless. Another new prop, and maybe a new shaft too if this one had taken too much punishment. John Fuller was going to be apoplectic.

"Well, gentlemen, I have to hand it to you, you do provide a certain element of the dramatic. Well, let's not just stand around. You've got your entire safari kit to unload as well as all those empty beer cans."

It took us nearly an hour to ferry the gear ashore in the Yelloweez, and by the time we were finished it was dark. A khaki mountain now stood by the water's edge. I went to get the Volvo.

It was too late to drive them to St.-Jean and then to return to the cottage. Since I planned to take Monday off from work anyway to deal with the Raven, I offered to lend them Di's Volvo.

"No way," said Paul before I even got the words out. "There's not the slightest chance I'll ever touch a piece of Gordon's machinery again!"

"Never mind," said Jim, grateful for the offer, "I'll drive."

Dinner was far from the celebratory scene I had envisaged. They pecked unenthusiastically at their steaks and Jim didn't take more than a sip of champagne because he was driving. Di did her best to cheer things up, but they just wanted to get going. She gave them a thermos of coffee as they went out the door.

"Remember, Jim, don't let Paul near that wheel," I joked as they left. They smiled weakly and drove off into the night. It was nearly midnight.

12

Raven Meets Raven

THERE WERE several marinas within striking distance of Thompson's Point, but the best for our purposes was the Marine Base at Essex Landing on the New York side. Essex Marine Base had the best mechanic and the best winter storage. The only problem was that in order to get there you had to take the ferry. Also, the mechanic was reputed to have a foul disposition.

Monday dawned fair, the last vestiges of the storm having dissipated. I phoned the marina and determined that Terence, the mechanic, would be available that morning.

"Di, I'm taking the Raven across to the marina. Should be through around lunch time. Why don't you drive over in the ferry with the kids and we can all have lunch in Essex and then we can drive back?"

"Sounds great to me. Doug can have another of those disgusting Coke floats they serve at the ice cream parlour."

"Yea-yea," said Doug.

The phone rang – at least it wouldn't be Fletcher. Wrong.

"Gordon, it's Jim. More bad news, I'm afraid."

"Oh no. Don't tell me you wrecked the Volvo?"

"Uh, well. We reached St.-Jean last night in good time and picked up my car at the marina. Paul refused to drive your Volvo unless I followed behind. So we drove in convoy all the way to the Champlain Bridge. That's where the trouble started."

"What trouble?"

"At the Champlain Bridge we had to part company because Paul lives on Nuns' Island in the opposite direction. Two in the morning, no way I was going to take the extra time to follow him all the way to his place."

"I can understand that."

"But Paul was absolutely adamant, so we had quite an argument. He wanted to keep my car and let me drive yours home. Didn't make any sense to me at all. So finally I drove off and left him standing there, cursing and shaking his fist."

"You did just what I'd have done, Jim. But why are you phoning to tell me all this?"

"Because when I got to my apartment the phone was ringing. It was Paul. No sooner had he started out toward Nuns' Island than your Volvo seized up."

"You've got to be kidding."

"No, really! Paul was fit to be tied! I had to go back and pick him up. We got a tow truck at three in the morning to take the car to the nearest garage. They've just determined the problem. Seems your water pump quit and the engine overheated. Fortunately there's no other damage."

"Well tell the people at the garage to go ahead and fix whatever needs fixing. And send me the towing bill. But Jim –"

"Yeah?"

"About Paul. Is he, uh, you know?"

"Oh Hell, he'll get over it. He's just mumbling and talking a lot of gibberish is all."

゚ッ ゚ッ ゚ッ

By the time the Raven and I reached Essex Landing I had a good idea what an egg must feel like being scrambled. She shook like a mechanical gravel sifter. I tied up at one of the docks and shakily went in search of the mechanic.

I found him, or more accurately his feet, deep in the bowels of a cruiser. He was adjusting something I couldn't see.

"Terence?"

There was no response. I thought he hadn't heard, so I cleared my throat.

"Uh, Terence?"

He wriggled half out and peered up at me, then went back to what he was doing.

I waited. He knew I was there, and presumably he knew how to speak, so there was little else I could do. I stood there for five minutes before he emerged, wiping his hands on a rag.

"You the guy with the wooden boat?" He glared at me with beady eyes.

"Yes. I'm the one who called this morning."

"Damn blueberry baskets, all of em! What kind you got?"

I pointed to the Raven.

"Century 22 foot inboard, 160 horse V8 Interceptor." I made the answer crisp, limited to essential information.

"Pile o' junk. Scrap it. Worse 'n a blueberry basket. Got another one the same in there." He jerked his head in the direction of the nearest shed. "Sinkin' all a time. What can I do for you?"

"Some friends were driving the boat yesterday and hit a reef. Prop's shot and maybe the shaft too."

"Leave 'er with me. I'll get to her eventually."

"When do you think that might be?"

There was a long pause while he glared at me some more. *Don't-you-realize-I'm-the-busiest-mechanic-on-the-lake-and-the-best-too-so-you-better-wait-your-turn?*

"Some time this week, I guess."

"Any chance she'll be fixed for the weekend? We're renting on the lake, and this will be our last weekend."

"See what I can do." *You-should-count-yourself-lucky-I'm-even-talking-to-you.*

"Thanks, Terence. Really appreciate it. Mind if I take a look at the other Raven?"

He grunted assent.

The other Raven was bathed in a bright light. Her hull was being attacked by a man with a drill – presumably he knew what he was doing. The whole surface below the waterline was peppered with white pimples where screws had been driven in and caulked.

"You're not by any chance Wally, are you?" I asked.

"That's me."

"I'm Gordon Green, owner of the other Raven."

"Yes, yes! Peter Regan's told me all about you! When's your boat arriving?"

"It's here, in a manner of speaking."

I told him of the latest mishap and of my meeting with the mechanic.

"Don't pay any mind to Terence. His bark's worse than his bite."

I stepped back and walked around the boat. It was eerie: the boat was identical to the Raven yet it wasn't the same. Same flat black hull, same toilet seat hatch . . . why did I get such different vibes? Was it the American eagle ornament on the bow, or Old Glory hanging from the stern? I didn't think so.

"I hear she's been having leaking problems, Wally."

"That's an understatement. Almost sank again last week in that storm. Water so rough I couldn't row out and bail her out."

"What seems to be the problem?"

"Old age, mostly. Nothing a surgeon's knife wouldn't fix, if I could afford it. But I try to get by this way," – he indicated the pox-ridden hull – "and in between times I give her the old sawdust treatment."

"The sawdust treatment?"

"Yeah. You make a little wooden trough, fill it with sawdust, drag it along the bottom of the boat while she's in the water. Sawdust rides up into all the cracks and swells. Stops the leaking like billy-be-damned. Only trouble is planks are forced further apart each year."

Something was troubling me. I saw in my mind's eye the Raven's rump swinging around, and this looked different. I could hear her raspberry of marine flatulence . . . that was it! The Raven's unique vocal quality came from twin exhausts, and this boat had only one.

"What kind of power does she have, Wally?"

"Chrysler straight six Crown Special, 135 horse."

"Mmmm, moves right along, I bet."

"Sure does. She'll go 27, 28 knots when she's feeling good. How about yours?

"A bit better than that because she has a V-8 Interceptor. But she's unpredictable as hell in the steering department."

"That so?"

"Tell you about it later, Wally – have to meet Di and the kids up by the office and I'm late. Go introduce yourself to the other Raven. She's down there at the dock needing sympathy."

That little visit gave me a lift. My Raven wasn't half bad, after all. Perhaps we could arrange a joint outing once the two Humpty-Dumpties had been put together again. I whistled as I walked up the slope to the marina office.

॰ঌ ॰ঌ ॰ঌ

I had to hold the phone from my ear. After John Fuller calmed down I gave him Terence's number, knowing the two would be a match for each other. I was right, for on Friday afternoon when I returned from Montreal the boat was all fixed and ready to go, new shaft and prop and all.

Saturday dawned sunny and warm, a perfect day for our first and only boating picnic of the season. We decided to try the Four Brother Islands for the picnic, for no other reason than they looked inviting on the chart. Nobody seemed to know much about them. They lay a mile off the New York shore, about eight miles up the lake from Essex.

Peter Regan shuttled us over to Essex to pick up the Raven. He and Gay couldn't join us for the picnic as they had other commitments later in the day, but Peter was keen to see the boat. The two Ravens bobbed heel to toe off the main dock. Old Glory was flying on Wally's boat, and to my surprise the Maple Leaf on ours. Who had put our flag up, I wondered? A stirring sight if ever there was one.

We pulled alongside and transferred picnic hamper, fishing gear and kids to our boat, then climbed aboard. I wore swimming trunks and Di had on her navy polka dot bikini. We didn't bother about a change of clothing as the weather was so warm. Just a small beach towel.

Wally appeared wearing a Maple Leaf flag in his hat and a Stars-and-Stripes T-shirt. He addressed me in his best Canadian accent.

"Hey, Gordon, eh? Glad to see you're oot and aboot. Hoo d'you like my handiwork? Hoop you don't mind, put yer flag up myself, eh?"

"Why, howdy, Wally," I reciprocated, trying to enter into the spirit of things, "sho' glad y'all hoisted that ol' banner on mah boat – she looks raht purdy."

Peter, on the point of leaving, winced. "Anyone would think this was the United Nations, flags and all. Wish I could hang around with you guys a bit longer, but I gotta go. Gay's waiting."

"Don't worry, Peter, the Raven fleet'll be around all summer. Thanks for the lift."

I turned to make introductions.

"Di, this is Wally. And Wally, that's Doug and that's Andy."

"Hi folks. So you're off on a picnic? Well, I'm going over to the other side of the lake, so why don't we leave in style?"

"Why not? Great idea."

He started his boat. It ran with a muffled purr, quite unlike the Raven's angry snarl. Wally looked round in surprise as I fired her up, then we made a stately two-abreast convoy out past the entry marker.

Wally opened his throttle and I stayed with him a few seconds, then dropped behind so I could show the Raven's true paces. When he was about 25 yards ahead I reached for the throttle, chuckling, and gave her everything she had. The Raven leapt ahead.

"Look at her eat up the open water, Di," I shouted. "This old Interceptor is fantas –"

A Messerschmidt dove down out of nowhere, engine screaming and guns blazing. A burst of rapid-fire detonations filled the air and the Raven stopped dead in the water, mortally wounded. The shocking silence was broken only by the lap of waves against her crippled side.

What started out as a morning of promise and national pride ended in the indignity of the Raven being towed back to the dock by her smooth-talking American cousin.

I ran up the dock to find Terence, who of course had gone off for the long weekend. By the time I got back to the boat Wally had departed and we were left high and dry, our only course to take the ferry back. We put the ravaged Raven to bed and bleakly schlepped picnic and fishing gear over to the ferry.

ॐ ॐ ॐ

Di huddled in a corner seat trying unsuccessfully to cover with the little beach towel what the bikini didn't.

"Jeedge I have never been so humiliated in all my life. Talk about disapproving looks – every woman on this ferry has given me the once-over. And you know that nice woman I was just talking to, the one who could have been a friend of Mom's?"

"You mean the one with the flowered hat over there?"

"Yes and don't stare. Know what she said?"

"No, what?"

"She said 'My dear, do you *always* travel dressed like that?' I tried my best to explain, but I know she didn't believe a word. I am totally humiliated."

Gay met us at the dock with sympathy and a cover-up, but from that day on it was open warfare between Di and the Raven. Di never trusted her again.

❧ ❧ ❧

I phoned Terence when I got back to Montreal.

"Terence, it's Gordon Green. More problems with the Raven, I'm afraid."

"I heard."

"Any idea what it could be?"

"Nope."

"Ever hear of an engine just blowing up like that before?"

"Yup. Coulda blowed a piston, throwed a rod, number a things."

"But what could cause that?"

"Dunno. Outa oil, maybe, or just plain old age."

"Well she wasn't out of oil, that much I do know," I said. "You only just changed the oil, remember?"

"Old age, then. Pile o' junk. I'll look at her when I get round to it, let you know."

He phoned next day. Curiosity had got the better of him.

"Crankshaft's broke clean in two."

"The *crankshaft?* Isn't that supposed to be the strongest part of the engine?"

"What they say."

"But Terence, what on earth could cause the crankshaft to shear like that? Could it have anything to do with the earlier accident?"

"Nah. Prop and shaft are like pieces of spaghetti compared to the crankshaft, absorb all the shock. Wouldn't have no effect on the crankshaft. Engine's a ol' piece a junk is all."

"But the engine's not *that* old – only about 18 years – and it doesn't have many hours. Why would it suddenly go like that? Have you ever heard of that happening before?"

"Nope."

"What do we do now?"

"Well you got three choices – or four, if you want to follow my advice and –"

"Terence . . ."

"Okay, so there's three things you can do. One, I can repair the motor myself, replace the crankshaft and main bearings. Two, you can buy a rebuilt short block. Three, you can buy a used motor. Don't buy a new one – just not worth it."

"Which do you recommend?"

"Reckon they each cost about the same, $1,500, give or take. My money, go for the short block. Comes with a guarantee, you know what you're gittin'. Trouble with repairin' your motor is we don't know what other damage we'll find once we git 'er all apart. Could be a sight more expensive by the time we're all finished. Same goes for the used engine – don't know what you're gittin'."

"What exactly is a short block?"

"Guts of the engine – engine block, pistons, valves and crankshaft. All rebuilt like new. We use the existing parts off your old engine for the rest."

"Makes sense to me. Leave it with me, Terence, I'll let you know."

I couldn't understand why the engine would simply blow apart like that. I started to ask around. No one had ever heard of a crankshaft shearing in that fashion without extreme stress due to some other factor.

The more I thought about it, the more I became convinced that the damage was related to the two previous high speed reef encounters. If this could be proven, then my insurance should cover the repairs. Terence be damned. I decided to test my theory out on a more reliable source – the engineering department at Interceptor Marine in Dearborn, Michigan.

I was put through to the engineering department and described my problem.

"Do you think," I asked in conclusion, "that the crankshaft could've sheared as the result of the two previous impacts?"

"How fast did you say you were going when you hit the reefs?"

"About 4000 RPM, say 30 knots."

"And the prop and shaft were damaged in each case?"

"Demolished is a better word."

"Well no crankshaft has yet been designed to withstand that kind of repeated punishment, particularly when it's in a high RPM, short stroke engine like your Interceptor 292. I'd say the shearing was almost certainly the result of the previous impacts."

"Would you be prepared to put that in writing?" I asked, trying to keep the excitement from my voice.

"Why, for insurance purposes?"

"Yes."

"No problem, be happy to."

I got his name, address and phone number. "I really appreciate this," I said. "I'm not sure yet if I need the letter, but I'll be back in touch if I do."

"Just let me know."

Armed with this information I phoned John Fuller.

"John, it's Gordon. I'm calling from Montreal. More problems, I'm afr –"

A muffled curse came from the other end, followed by a click and a dial tone.

I looked at the receiver in my hand. All things considered, I could hardly blame John for hanging up on me. But I gave him the benefit of the doubt and called back. He answered on the first ring.

"Gordon, that you? Sorry – I've been having problems with my phone. Keeps cutting out just after the other party starts speaking. You probably thought I hung up on you, hah-hah."

"Now John, why ever would I think such a thing?"

"Just joking. So you have more problems?"

"Putting it mildly."

I took him through the crankshaft incident, chapter and verse, including my discussion with Terence and the conflicting conclusions of the Interceptor engineer. He didn't interrupt once.

"So you see, I can't *prove* that the breakage was caused by the two previous impacts. But to me it's perfectly obvious that it was – in fact it's stretching the imagination to think otherwise. And I can produce a letter from an expert who backs that opinion, Terence's view notwithstanding."

There was a long silence. Then John surprised me.

"That letter won't be necessary, Gordon. Based on what you've told me, I'll recommend to the insurance company that they settle for replacement cost. But this will have to be confirmed by the insurance adjuster, and I'm afraid you'll have to pay a second deductible as it's a separate though related incident."

The insurance adjuster asked me to prepare an accident report outlining the nature of the damage. I cited the already reported Pointe-au-Fer incident as the cause of the broken crankshaft, and appended a schedule detailing the costs of repair under the three alternatives. The repair work using the short block was quickly approved.

ॐ ॐ ॐ

My success as an engineering sleuth inspired me to try to get to the bottom of the Raven's bizarre steering behaviour. I called back the engineer at Interceptor.

"You say it only happens under certain conditions, and usually at near maximum revs?"

"That's right, and it's always when I'm turning to port, never to starboard."

"Hmm. The relationship between prop, rudder and hull at that speed is quite complex. Have you spoken to the people at Century?"

"To be honest that never occurred to me. Century doesn't make wooden boats any more – all fibreglass, mostly inboard/outboards. My boat's nearly 20 years old."

"Well, without seeing the original design I can't be much help to you. Why don't you try contacting them? Maybe one of their old timers is still around."

My initial contact at Century was not encouraging.

"Don't think there's anyone here can help, sir, not in this department anyway. But wait a minute. Hey, Rod! Know anyone was around here in 1958? Anyone on the shop floor? Yeah, old Craig – yeah. Hold on a minute, sir, I'll transfer you to Craig. He may be able to help you."

Craig had worked for Century most of his life and remembered the 22-foot Raven well.

"That's the model with two chrome-trimmed fish tank hatches on the stern, right?"

"You've got it – and the toilet seat hatch cover."

He laughed. "Never thought of it that way, but now you mention it, that's a good one! Anyway, what seems to be the problem?"

"She goes hard to starboard when I turn to port."

"All the time?"

"No – only when she's near maximum revs and I'm already starting the turn. The harder I pull the wheel over, the sharper she turns in the opposite direction."

"And you have a 160 hp Interceptor for power, right?"

"How'd you know?"

He laughed again. "The old cavitation problem! A design flaw if ever there was one. We had to modify a bunch of them that year, but couldn't reach all the owners. Your boat being in Canada probably got missed."

"What was the problem?"

"With the particular power/prop pitch combination in that Interceptor, we located the prop too far aft. At high speeds the prop would start sucking in air from beyond the transom, causing what is known as cavitation. This deflected the thrust away from the rudder and resulted in extremely erratic steering."

"What's the cure?"

"Simply fool the prop into thinking there's another three inches of hull over it. Best way's to make an L-shaped plate, say six inches vertical, three horizontal, about eight inches wide. Screw the vertical part to the transom, making sure the three-inch bottom of the L is flush with the bottom of the hull. That's all there is to it."

"You mean a little piece of metal just three inches out from the transom can make all that difference?"

"That's right. Fixed a bunch myself."

"Craig, you've made my day. Thanks for all your help."

ॐ ॐ ॐ

Peter Regan worked for Hazlett Corp., an innovative engineering company that designed and manufactured equipment for continuous casting of bronze and other base metals. I asked Peter if his machine shop could make up the plate I needed.

"You'll have to get the precise measurements, Gordon – your boat's not all square edges."

The Raven's bottom was indeed rounded and the transom was curved, not square. I made a template of the complex shape and dropped it off at Peter's house.

"There's no rush on this, Peter. The boat won't even be in the water until next summer."

"Well you better have those steering problems fixed by then. Gay and I are counting on that promised picnic. And tell Di to have her bikini ready."

ॐ ॐ ॐ

Terence completed the engine repair work and I forwarded a copy of his bill to John Fuller. Fuller's reply and cheque came by return mail –

he must have been afraid that something else might go wrong if he didn't settle promptly:

JOHN FULLER & ASSOCIATES LTD.

Mr. Gordon Green
165 Edghill Road
Westmount, P.Q.

Dear Gordon:

Re. Century Engine Repairs

I enclose our cheque for $1,827.65, being the Canadian dollar equivalent of the cost of the repairs to your engine, less the deductible. Please sign and return the enclosed release at your earliest convenience.

In future, I strongly suggest you limit your boating activities to the bathtub.

Sincerely,
John Fuller

13

A Cussed Mechanic

THE QUEBEC WINTER of 1977/78 seemed endless. We enrolled the kids in a junior ski program at Mont St. Sauveur but yearned for the summer months. When spring finally came we learned to our delight that the Sillcox cottage was available again. In late June I phoned Terence and asked him to dewinterize and launch the Raven.

"If I do, she won't be afloat when you git here."

"How so, Terence?"

"She's punky all around the exhaust ports. Needs a new plank on the transom. Noticed it last fall when I was fixin' the motor."

"So why didn't you tell me this last fall? We've had all winter to fix her up."

"Costs plenty to call Montreal, not worth it for that ol' heap. Shoulda axed."

I counted to ten. Terence wanted nothing more than for me to explode at him over the phone.

"What do you suggest we do now?"

"I'll caulk her up best I can. Should last till fall. Fix the transom next winter."

"All right, Terence, you go ahead and do that, and scrape and paint the bottom, dewinterize the motor and the rest. I'll come by a week Saturday."

⚓ ⚓ ⚓

On the way to Thompson's Point I dropped by Peter Regan's to pick up the steel plate. The Hazlett shop had used sturdy 3/16-inch stainless steel that would last a lifetime. They had drilled and countersunk the screwholes where the gently curved plate would be attached to the Raven's transom, and had even provided the screws. It was a work of art. You couldn't even detect the seams where the components of the complex shape had been welded together. They charged me a fraction of what it must have cost in shop time.

Next morning I picked up the Raven and brought her to the shallow water off the beach where I could work on her. I left the motor idling to charge the battery which seemed low.

I positioned the plate over the Raven's rump and held it there with my right hand. It fit like a glove, the curved steel hugging exactly to the contour of the transom. I could feel the soft, sensuous vibrations of the idling motor through the palm of my hand; for once she didn't swing away. I marked the screwholes with an awl, drilled holes for the screws with a hand drill, and attached the shiny plate.

I couldn't wait to try her out. I pushed out into deeper water, scrambled aboard and headed out to the centre of the lake. Terence had warned me to let the rebuilt engine run a few hours before opening her right up, but even at 3000 RPM I could tell the difference. The Raven responded eagerly in either direction: gone was the favouring of the starboard turn, and in no way could I simulate the Bensfort Bridge syndrome.

More amazing, she had suddenly acquired low speed steering. The extra piece of "hull" aft of the prop directed the thrust right at the little rudder, the way it was supposed to. Why had it taken me three years to discover this?

Elated, I headed back to the mooring. I felt I had an entirely new boat. Only after I tied up did I notice water seeping over the floorboards.

It turned out the cotton waste material in the rudder stuffing box had dried out and shrunk over the winter, allowing water to pour in around the rudder shaft. As soon as I tightened the tamping nut the leaking stopped. But I didn't have the right tools to tighten the main lock nut properly, so I made a mental note to speak to Terence about that.

The volume of water that had leaked into the boat would explain the low battery, since the automatic bilge pump would have been working overtime just to keep her afloat. To be on the safe side, I double checked the mercury float switch on the automatic bilge pump. It was working fine.

Next day we had our first picnic. I loaded the family including the dog into the dinghy (Eloise in the Yelloweez – Andy loved that) and ferried them to the boat. We crossed over to the New York side and headed south until we came to a sheltered bay where we dropped anchor.

The New York shore south of Essex is composed of ancient granite, quite different from the sedimentary shale of Thompson's Point, more like the Muskokas, or even Georgian Bay. The smooth pink-gray granite was warm to the feet, and the water sparkled in the sunlight. Stunted white pines and scrub oak competed for scant foothold in a pungent tapestry of bonsai artistry. I later learned that even the Mississauga rattlesnake, familiar to Georgian Bay and Muskoka cottagers, makes its home on those shores.

We spread out our lunch on the rock and luxuriated in the reflected warmth. Peanut butter and jelly sandwiches for the kids, smoked salmon and cream cheese for us, and a Heineken for good measure, topped off by Sarah Lee orange cake.

"This really is a perfect spot, Di, so close to Thompson's Point and not another soul in sight." I reached for another beer. "Wonder what the fishing's like?"

"Why don't you give it a try?"

The kids' fishing rod was in the boat. I put on a sinking Rappala, cast out to the middle of the channel and let it sink a bit before reeling in. Within seconds I had something big on the end.

"Doug, come quick! I've got something!"

Doug took the rod and started to play the fish.

"Tip up, Doug! Keep the tip up, or he'll shake loose! Keep the tension on the line, but don't wind too fast! Let him run if he wants to, that's the way!" I was more excited than he was.

With incessant clucking from me Doug managed to play the fish up to the boat where I netted it. The pickerel weighed in at just under five pounds. It was a proud moment for father and son.

Later that afternoon we swam in the warm clear water off the sloping rock. We donned masks and snorkels and looked for more fish. We cavorted and splashed and dove, then went home and ate fresh pickerel fillets and local baby potatoes. It was that kind of a day. I didn't even think once about the Raven's leaking.

᭡ ᭡ ᭡

Sunday I took my early morning swim on the beach side of the point where the Raven was moored. I swam out to her and was about to grab the rail when she swung her stern around. I hoped no one was watching.

I clambered aboard and checked the rudder stuffing box. The tamping nut had loosened during the previous day's outing and she was leaking. To confirm that fact, the automatic bilge pump kicked in and stayed pumping for a couple of minutes. I retightened the tamping nut, then started the motor and left her idling to charge the battery while I went to get breakfast.

This leaking disturbed me. The battery had now become the finger in the dyke, the only thing between the Raven and the bottom. And since I wasn't planning my vacation until mid-July, I wouldn't be around during the week to cope. And Di had sworn to have nothing to do with the Raven.

After breakfast I shut off the motor. The leaking had stopped and the battery seemed fully charged. I asked Tom Robertson, a neighbour whose cottage overlooked the bay, to keep an eye on the Raven during the week.

᭡ ᭡ ᭡

I phoned Terence from the office and asked him to tighten the locknut when he was next on the Vermont side.

"Ain't gonna touch that boat less it's here under our direct care. We don't have no insurance for that kinda thing. You could sue me."

Some people are born with a truly black soul and take no end of delight in causing discomfort in others. What drives these individuals to behave so adversely? Is it a repressed childhood? Feelings of inadequacy? Sexual impotence?

"Come on, Terence, we're just talking about a lousy lock nut. All I'm asking is you check her when you're over on that side."

᭙ ᭙ ᭙

Friday morning Tom Robertson called.

"Gordon, your boat nearly sank this morning."

"Good Lord, Tom, what happened?"

"Well, she seemed pretty low in the water yesterday afternoon. I was about to take your dinghy out to check when I saw that mechanic guy from Essex pull up in his boat. He got aboard so I assumed everything was okay. Then when I looked this morning she was almost up to the gunwales."

"Good grief. I'm so sorry you had to go through this. I suppose you had to go out to her."

"Yes, well, that was no problem. The battery was under water and flatter'n a pancake. I got a spare one and borrowed some jumper cables and hooked it up to your pump and she's fine now, but I don't know how long that'll last. She's pumping all the time – pump switch seems stuck."

"I owe you big, Tom, really big. Hope you don't mind keeping an eye on her till I get down there this afternoon. I'm leaving right after lunch."

᭙ ᭙ ᭙

"Terence it's Gordon Green. My boat nearly sank this morning."

"Uh-huh."

"Someone saw you checking her out yesterday afternoon."

"Uh-huh."

"They said she was pretty low in the water, but when they saw you there they assumed everything was okay."

"Well they shouldn't of."

"How so, Terence?"

"Told you about legal liability. Damn blueberry basket was sinkin', nuttn' I could do."

"Couldn't you have phoned me?"

"What good would that do? Boat's here, you're there. Can't babysit everyone."

It seemed this man's cussedness knew no bounds. Only the quiet decorum of the Morgan Stanley offices prevented me from jumping down the phone and throttling him. But Terence was the best mechanic around.

"Terence I'm really disappointed you couldn't even go to the effort of notifying somebody that the boat had problems. My elderly neighbour had to paddle out there this morning with a spare battery and jumper cables to pump her out. And don't start on about legal liability – it's just pure human decency we're talking about here."

There was a long silence after which Terence surprised me.

"Jeez I didn't figure she'd git any worse. Knew you'd be here later today to deal with her. Bring her over tomorrow we'll git the stuffin' box fixed."

He sounded almost chagrined. This was the closest to an apology I ever received from Terence.

⚓ ⚓ ⚓

I bought a set of top quality heavy duty jumper cables at an automotive supply outlet just outside Burlington.

"Tom, I can't tell you how much I appreciate your help. I picked up these for you as you obviously don't have any."

"You didn't have to do that, Gordon," he laughed, "I don't suppose I'll ever need them again – that is, unless you plan to make a habit of this! But I appreciate this and I'll keep them on hand. By the way, I took your battery out and had it recharged. It's in the garage."

As I rowed out to the Raven I could hear the bilge pump working away. Enough water was burping through the system to keep the pump impeller wet but she was obviously pumping on an empty bilge.

The noise stopped when I disconnected Tom's borrowed jumper cables. I transferred the spare battery and cables to the Yelloweez, then turned the manual/auto/off switch to the "off" position and hooked up the recharged battery. The pump stayed off. But when I switched to "automatic" the pump started up again at full speed even though the bilge was empty. Puzzled, I lifted the hatch to examine the mercury float switch. It was stuck in the upright position.

A mercury float switch just isn't supposed to stick like that. It is a critical failsafe device on any boat. It's designed so that it cannot ever jam in the "on" position and run down the battery. Yet here was this insignificant contraption standing at full attention, defying gravity. I gently touched it with my finger and it flopped down and switched off the pump. I tried to jam it up again but it wouldn't stay. Whatever had caused that switch to stick was something very subtle. As I knelt there scratching my head, a prolonged gurgle came from the Raven's exhaust ports. It had a rhythm like a deep belly laugh.

꙳ꙮ ꙳ꙮ ꙳ꙮ

I lay awake that night pondering how to prevent the float switch from jamming again and finally hit on a solution. I would install a second mercury float switch in series with the first, so that both switches would have to be in the upright position for the unit to switch on. The odds against both switches accidentally jamming open at the same time were so remote as to be virtually impossible.

Next morning I took the boat over to Terence. He tightened the leaking rudder post and stopped the leaking completely. Proudly I produced a second float switch and explained how I wanted it installed. Terence was unimpressed.

"Pump's gonna quit she'll quit," he said as he crimped the last piece of wire together. "All this fancy wirin' ain't gonna help one bit."

I thanked Terence for his time and encouragement and set off back to Thompson's Point.

14

Unfair Game

ONE AUGUST WEEKEND in 1979 we invited the Taylors for a family picnic on the New York side of the lake. The weather was hot and muggy: possible thunderstorms were forecast. Jim and Lyn's station wagon disgorged two picnic hampers, a large cooler, three kids, a babysitter and two Yorkshire terriers. With our two kids and Eloise we numbered ten, plus the three dogs.

I ferried troops, animals and supplies out to the Raven. All wore bathing suits. I counted heads and life jackets and cast a dubious eye to the sky – still no clouds, but the air was heavy, unsettled like a queasy stomach.

The secluded little harbour on the New York side of the lake where Doug had earlier landed the pickerel seemed an ideal picnic spot. It was only a 15-minute run from Thompson's Point and if the weather turned nasty we could make a run for it. We rounded the point into the bay and nosed into shore to unload. We had the place to ourselves. There wasn't a breath of wind. Heat radiated from the ancient granite, and the air was heavy with the aroma of pine pitch and juniper berries. We spread out the picnic on the smooth rock.

"Now," said Jim, rubbing his hands as the kids headed off to swim, "how about a little libation before lunch?" He opened the cooler he had cradled on his lap on the way across. "Ice cold chablis, anyone?"

"Ah, Taylor, you do travel in style." I settled back against a stunted white pine.

He set out four plastic wine glasses on the rock and filled the glasses.

"A steady hand, James. Now tell me this isn't nature in the raw. What could be more elemental than sitting on bedrock smoothed by ancient glaciers and warmed by the sun, quaffing ice-cold wine from a plastic chalice?"

"Chablis on the rocks," said Lyn.

We toasted Mother Nature, savouring the sibilating silence. A cicada joined in the applause.

"You know, the last time we were here Doug landed a nice pickerel – or walleye as you probably call it."

"Really? Where did he hook it?" Jim was a keen fisherman.

"Right there, in the middle of the channel, about opposite the boat. I'll show you."

I put down my glass and dove into the lake. The water was cool and refreshing. Dripping, I pulled the Raven in by the bowline and stepped aboard. The kids' fishing rod was still rigged with a sinking Rappala. I cast out and just as the lure landed a small boat entered the bay. I started to reel in.

The approaching boat contained two officers in uniform, evidently game wardens. All manner of things went through my mind. We were on the New York side of the lake and I didn't have a New York State fishing licence. Moreover my Vermont licence was in my wallet, and my wallet was back at Thompson's Point. I decided that nonchalance was the best course.

"Morning, fellas" I said brightly, bringing the line in and casting out again.

"Any luck?" the one in front asked.

"Not yet. That was my first cast."

"Uh-huh. Well let's see your fishin' licence."

"Fishing licence? I, er, that is, it's back at the house."

"Oh? And where's that?"

"Back over there," I pointed across the lake, "near Charlotte."

"In Vermont, huh? Hey, Dave, says his licence's in Vermont. Bet he ain't even got a New York licence. You got a New York State fishin' licence, sonny?"

This was a decidedly unfriendly beginning.

"A New York State licence? You mean I need a *separate* licence for fishing on this side of the lake?"

By this time the kids had gathered to witness the interrogation and the officers were playing to a full house. The wardens beached their boat and climbed out. I noticed that one of them, the one called Dave, wore a gun.

"Let's see your driver's licence, sonny."

"My driver's licence is with my fishing licence, and that's in my wallet back at the house."

"Okay well let's see your boat registration, then."

"I don't have any on the boat."

"No boat registration?" He immediately looked suspicious. "You're supposeta have boat registration."

"The boat's registered in Canada," I explained, "and the registration papers are in my files back in Montreal."

"Now wait a minute. You said you lived in Vermont."

"Officer, I live in Montreal, and we've rented a cabin in Vermont for the summer. These are my friends and family. We've all come over here for a picnic. Now if I've done something wrong fishing here without a New York State licence, then please issue me a ticket so we can get on with our picnic."

"Waddya think, Dave?" my chief interrogator continued, "No driver's licence, no boat registration, he could just skip back to Montreal and we never hear from him again. No, we'll just havta book him, that's all, he'll havta come with us, right?"

"Right," said the one called Dave, "gotta book him, take him ta local court."

"Now wait a minute," I said, "you can't just take me away like that! I can't leave these people, the weather's threatening. Here, why don't you take this as security?" I offered the little fishing rod. "You're welcome to keep it until I come in and pay my fine on Monday."

"Nope. Ya could just as easy skip town. You're comin' with us."

"But this is ridiculous. No one else here knows how to drive this boat. And thunderstorms are forecast. This could be life-threatening."

"Shoulda thoughta that before ya broke the law."

What a power trip! Short of outright defying them – and given their arsenal I didn't relish the consequences of that – I had no option but to go with them.

"Anyone got any money? I don't have a red cent with me."

Jim and Lyn both shrugged, as did Di.

"Here's 60 dollars," said the babysitter, reaching into her bikini top and producing three crispy twenties. I opened my mouth to speak, then closed it again and gratefully took the notes. I stuffed them into my bathing suit pocket and climbed into the outboard.

"Keep the wine on ice, Jim," I called out.

"Don't worry, Green, there's another bottle where that came from."

As we put-putted away, Jim let his movie camera roll. I stood up, crossed my arms at the wrists in invisible handcuffs and raised them over my head, lowering them slowly. This act of defiance was not appreciated by my captors. They refused to speak to me directly. All communication was now conveyed through their two-way dialogue.

"Where are you taking me?"

"I'd say this guy's in real trouble, Joe. You done right to book him like that. We'll get the magistrate in Westport deal with him."

Westport was about five miles down the lake. We tied up at the town dock and set out to find the local magistrate. I felt ridiculous, traipsing around in my wet bathing suit with a couple of goons dressed to kill. Half an hour had already passed since my arrest and I was anxious about the families left on the rock. Unfortunately this was the weekend of the annual Westport country fair; hundreds of people were milling about. The magistrate was finally located fast asleep under an apple tree, a half-empty case of beer beside him. The officers decided that discretion was called for and they moved on.

They escorted me to their car, an official sedan with a crest on the door and a wire grille separating front from back like a police cruiser. Opening the back door and dramatically reaching in front of me, Joe removed a rifle and deposited it in the front seat. He motioned me in back.

"I'd like to know where you're taking me, please."

He slammed the door and ignored me. We drove about five miles inland until we reached a police station just near Interstate Highway 87.

An imposing lawn stretched from the station to the road; Old Glory flew atop a flagpole in the middle of the lawn. Evidently all the police were attending the fair as well, for the place was deserted.

"Don't look like nobody's here neither, Dave. We better go in use the radio." They disappeared into the building.

The minutes ticked by. The lawn looked inviting, so I tested the door and it opened. I went over to the flagpole and lay down. The sun was warm on my face . . .

"Hey, you! What you think you're doin'? Jesus, Joe, the guy's tryin' ta excape!"

Joe came running out of the station. I sat up slowly.

"You stay put, sonny, ya hear?"

"Why won't you tell me what you're doing?"

"He wants to know what we're doin', Dave. Maybe we should tell him the law says if ya can't find a magistrate in one place then ya gotta go to the next nearest place, and if there's not one there, ya just keep goin'."

"I just don't believe this. You're taking this thing too far. There are a lot of people I'm responsible for out there. Human lives could be at stake."

"Just get back in that car, sonny."

He came toward me, hands at his sides. I retreated to the car with as much dignity as I could muster. He slammed the door after me.

"Reckon we'll try Elizabethtown next, Dave. If there's no one there, may havta go all the way to Lake Placid."

They found the magistrate in Elizabethtown, about five miles further up the road. From his appearance I guessed the kindly man had been awakened from his afternoon nap.

"Mr. Green, you have been charged with angling in New York State waters without the requisite angler's licence. How plead you?"

"How serious is this charge, your Honour?"

He looked at me and winked. "Not very serious."

"Then I plead Guilty, your Honour."

He banged his gavel. "The accused has pleaded Guilty and will be fined 25 dollars." He turned with a smile. "That will be 25 dollars, please."

I reached into my bathing suit pocket and felt something squishy. I carefully withdrew three waterlogged 20-dollar bills and smoothed two of them out on the bench. The magistrate went into his chambers to get change and asked the two officers to join him. I couldn't hear what transpired, but voices were raised and Joe and Dave emerged looking chastened. Not a word was exchanged on the return trip.

It was nearly three o'clock when we finally got back. I was starving and could already taste the chablis. A cheer went up as we pulled into view, and I rose to my feet and clenched my hands over my head in a victory salute. My captors glowered.

Di ran down and threw her arms around me. "Oh Jeedge we were worried. Where have you been all this time?"

"You won't believe me. We had to go all the way to Elizabethtown to find a magistrate. My friends there" - I motioned toward the departing outboard - "are a couple of real dicks. But enough – I'll tell you more later. Right now I'm starved, and in need of liquid sustenance. Taylor, pull that cork!"

There was an awkward silence.

"Uh, Gordon, we didn't think you'd be gone that long, so we opened the second bottle in preparation for your return, and – well – we didn't want the wine to get too warm, you understand . . ."

"What Jim's saying is there's no more wine. We drank it all," said Lyn.

"Well darling now, come on, it wasn't quite like that. It just sort of happened."

"Hey, guys, so what? Don't all stand there with such long faces! Wine's gone, it's spilt milk, so we celebrate with beer!"

I couldn't have cared less. The Bud tasted as good as the finest vintage chablis and Di's sandwiches were great.

15

Winds of Change

THE SEASON drew rapidly to a close and we now sadly contemplated leaving Thompson's Point. We didn't think the Sillcoxes wanted to rent the next summer, and things were happening on the political and professional fronts that made us reconsider whether we should continue to live in Quebec.

On the last week of rental I was pulled out of a meeting at the office to take an urgent call from Di.

"Jeedge you've got to come right down. Your boat's up on the rocks."

"My God. How could that happen?"

"I have no idea. All I know is your precious mistress is on the rocks at the east end of the bay, and the wind is blowing from the south and she's taking a pounding. You'll have to come right down here."

"Okay, Di, listen to me. Try to find somebody who has a boat to pull her off, or put out an anchor, or whatever. Just try to find some able bodies. I'll be there as fast as I possibly can."

I broke all records driving down. The roads were strangely deserted – I was used to the weekend rush. By the time I got there the wind had dropped and the Raven hung limply at anchor off the shore, still attached to her now useless mooring buoy.

Di had rounded up a group of Thompson's Point teenagers who had physically held the boat off the rocks while the anchor was rowed out as far as possible. They then pulled her out to the anchor. I could see her bow had been badly scarred, but the damage was superficial. She wasn't leaking at all.

"Di, ask the crew if they want to join us for lunch in Shelburne. I'll take the Raven out to deeper water – if the wind comes up again her anchor'll never hold on that bedrock. Won't be long."

I rowed out to the Raven and pulled up the trailing mooring line. The end was like a frayed mop. The splice which had been around the thimble was chewed right through, and presumably the thimble now lay on the bottom, still attached to the chain.

It wasn't hard to deduce what had happened. The end of the heavy anchor chain normally rested on the bedrock, but as soon as the wind came up the Raven would pull on the mooring and snap the chain off the bottom. In between waves the chain would flop back, banging the spliced nylon rope against the abrasive bedrock. Every time this happened a little more rope would be chewed away, until finally it parted.

I remembered that the marina had urged me to use all chain for the mooring anchor line. I had been too penny-pinching to follow their advice.

❧ ❧ ❧

The winds of change blew stronger. As winter approached, a spring referendum on the question of Quebec separation seemed inevitable. Opinion was divided on whether it would succeed, and we were nervous of the potential effect on property values.

On the professional front, working for a U.S. firm had its drawbacks, too. The work was still challenging, and I had the greatest respect for Morgan Stanley; but I was weary of being treated as a pariah by the Canadian investment community. A foreigner in my own country, barred for purely political reasons from doing business in Toronto, its financial centre.

For two years I had negotiated with Jim Baillie, then Chairman of the Ontario Securities Commission, to allow Morgan Stanley, a non-resident controlled firm, to move its office to Toronto. We had finally been given the green light, no mean achievement, but now my New York boss (who owned a farm in Vermont which he visited after his frequent Friday visits to the Montreal office) gave only lip-service to my initiative. The foot-dragging could go on indefinitely.

Time was of the essence. If the referendum became a reality, the effect on property values could be immediate and devastating. I began to think in terms of changing jobs. I was nervous that I might not quickly find a suitable position with another firm in Toronto, but I was even more concerned that we could lose much of the large investment we had in our Montreal house.

We consulted realtors, and in January 1980 we put our house on the market, setting the price about 25% above the price we had paid in 1975. I told myself we were just putting our toe in the water. If there was no action within a month we could lower the price if the threatened referendum seemed closer to reality.

Two days after the house was listed we received a stink bid. We rejected that, but the same bidder returned the next day with an all cash offer only $10,000 below the asking price. We countered at $5,000 below and he accepted.

I was flabbergasted. I had expected to weigh all our options and plan the career change with careful deliberation. Now we had nowhere to live as of the end of April, and I had no job.

༈ ༈ ༈

I didn't have to worry about the job. It turned out that my years of experience at Morgan Stanley were attractive to a number of Canadian firms, and there was no scarcity of offers. But the firm I knew best and had worked with most closely was Dominion Securities. That firm was just turning the corner, after several years of decline, under the youthful leadership of Tony Fell. I knew a number of the DS senior people well, and we quickly worked out a deal.

The timing of my move to DS was fortunate. Within a year of my joining DS, under Tony's leadership the firm had broken out from the crowd; several mergers later it was the dominant firm in Canada. I stayed with DS for the rest of my career.

We found a house in Rosedale, that park-like residential area of trees and ravines located conveniently close to downtown Toronto. We were shocked by the price differential between Toronto and Montreal housing, and had to mortgage our futures to complete the purchase.

The Raven still lay in dry dock at the Essex Marine Base. Di was adamant. The severed mooring line was the final nail in the coffin. She insisted I get rid of the boat.

"Di, that mooring let go as a result of my own stupidity. You can't blame that on the Raven."

"I don't care, I'm sick of the endless dramas. That boat costs nothing but money and it's always breaking down. Where do you think you're going to keep it when we get to Rosedale – on the front lawn? Perhaps you could grow petunias in it."

Di had a point. We had no plans to buy a cottage at that time, and the boat had never looked prettier. It was a good time to sell, before the next round of rot set in.

Feeling like Judas Iscariot, I contacted a Burlington yacht broker and listed the Raven. I phoned Terence and asked him to show the boat when requested, promising him a 5% commission when the boat sold. The asking price was U.S. $4,500.

Then I became preoccupied with the move back to Toronto and my new duties at DS. I didn't think of the Raven again until the fall when I called the broker.

"Funny thing you should call, Mr. Green, we were just talking about your Century this morning. Quite a few people have gone over to Essex to look at the boat, but not one of them has called back. Are you sure the boat's as you describe it?"

"I'm pretty sure it is, unless something's happened I don't know about. Why don't you see if you can track down one of the people who went to see her, ask him what the story is?"

Then I phoned Terence.

"Terence, the broker tells me he's sent several people over to see the Raven."

"Uh-huh."

"Did they show any interest?"

"Nope."

"Well did they look the boat over? I mean, did you take them in and show it to them?"

"Boat's in the back. See fer themselves."

"I see. Well now, Terence, I would really like to sell this boat, so I appreciate any help you can give to show her at her best advantage."

There was silence.

"Terence?"

"Yup."

"Can I count on your help?"

"Right sucker comes along, he'll buy."

I counted to ten. "All right, Terence, nothing's going to happen over the winter months. I'll decide what we should do next April." And hung up.

A couple of days later the broker called.

"Mr. Green, I just spoke to the last party went down to see your boat. They took the ferry from Burlington to Port Kent then drove all the way down to Essex to see this Terence character. He told them they were wasting their time, kept telling them it was a blueberry basket! They insisted on taking a look anyway, but it was so dark in the shed they couldn't see anything. The boat was jammed in the back, and Terence didn't offer any assistance, so they left."

I decided to move the boat to Burlington in the spring.

⚓ ⚓ ⚓

The Toronto winter reluctantly released its grip. In April the warmer weather stirred our yearning to be on the water. We enquired about a place to rent on Georgian Bay and learned that the Campbell place at the entrance to Go-Home Bay was for rent. This familiar landmark, sitting atop a rocky outcrop, was large with plenty of water frontage. We rented the place sight unseen for the month of July.

As with all Go-Home properties, the half-hour run to and from Honey Harbour required a good-sized boat. And so it was that the intended sale of the Raven never took place. With Terence standing guardian at the gate and ourselves now needing a boat, the compelling forces of reason could not be denied.

16

Bartering with Tenderloin

"LOOK AT IT THIS WAY, Di," I said, trying to sound sympathetic, "we need a boat this summer. To buy a new one would cost a fortune. We already own the Raven, so it won't cost us anything, and at least we know her, faults and all."

"That is an understatement."

"Look, love. She has a virtually new motor, and the hull's in pretty good shape. Let's at least bring her out here and use her for the summer. Then we can decide in the fall if we want to sell her, when we'll be close by."

"All very logical, but just how do you plan to bring her out? I haven't heard that Jim Fletcher's sitting on the edge of his seat awaiting your call."

"Seriously, Doug and I have been talking about it, haven't we, Doug? It will be a wonderful trip for us both."

"You must be joking. If Fletcher and Spafford ran her aground three times, you and Doug'd double that. And where do you think you'd get the time to make this grand journey?"

"Not by water! Doug and I would drive to Essex to pick her up on her original trailer that's still in Honey Harbour. Drive her back over the Adirondacks, do it all over a long weekend."

A smile lit across her features. "Hmm. You'll take Doug off my hands for a whole weekend? Now *that's* a deal."

"Aw, c'mon, Mom!"

"What do you say, Doug, let's go get the map out and plan our route."

⚓ ⚓ ⚓

We decided to drive out the boring way – Trans Canada Highway to Montreal, then south down the west side of Lake Champlain to Essex. On the way back we would retrace our steps as far as Plattsburgh but then cut west over the Adirondack Mountains to Malone, N.Y. and thence to the bridge at Cornwall, Ontario, where we would rejoin the Trans Canada Highway. Doug was only 12 so I would do all the driving.

The Raven was solid mahogany and heavy. We needed a powerful vehicle with a good trailer hitch, and Paul Henderson, Olympic sailor and supporter of all things nautical, graciously lent us his van. He frequently used it to haul sailing boats around and it was perfect for the purpose.

⚓ ⚓ ⚓

It was a sparkling early May morning and there was little traffic. High in the cab of the van I watched the sun rise over fields still brown from winter, slanting its golden rays, promising warmth. The two-hour drive went by quickly, and soon we were in Honey Harbour, hitching up the tandem trailer.

"Hop in the van, Mr. Green, and pump the brakes. That's it – brake lights are working fine. Now try the turn signals. Great! And the headlights – okay, the tail lights are on. Checked the brakes on the trailer and they're working too. Greased all the bearings, but you should stop frequently anyway and feel if any of the wheels are hot. Never know when one of the little devils is ready to go."

I hastily acknowledged his prophetic advice and bade him thanks and adieu. We had much territory to cover.

❧ ❧ ❧

A service station on the highway near Belleville, about 100 miles east of Toronto, served us a flying hotdog. It was not yet two o'clock.

"This is great, Doug. At this rate we should reach Montreal by six this evening, right on schedule."

"Dad?"

"Uh-huh?"

"Next time could we eat a little sooner? And have something more for breakfast than just toast? I was starving."

"Oh Doug, I've been so wrapped up in making our schedule that I forgot all about our stomachs. We'll stop somewhere near Montreal and have a good supper. Promise."

We hit the tail of the Montreal rush hour traffic and took nearly an hour to bypass the city. Then we drove some distance south until we found an inviting looking restaurant just off the highway. We both ordered steak.

I was flagging badly. It soon became obvious that we shouldn't try to reach Essex that evening, so we pulled into the first motel we could find after Plattsburgh and called it a day.

❧ ❧ ❧

We found Terence working on a cruiser in the storage shed by the water, in the familiar position.

"Morning Terence," I said to his feet.

"Whoog foo?" A hollow muffle came from the bowels of the cruiser.

"It's Gordon."

"Woothoo ray way."

Doug jabbed me in the ribs. "Dad, what's with that guy?"

"Nothing, a little unusual is all. He'll come out in about five minutes, you'll see."

Terence emerged on schedule, wiping his hands.

"Hi Terence, you remember Doug?"

Terence lit his beady eyes on Doug. "Growed a bit, enny?"

"Doug's helping me drive her back. Is she all set to go? Didn't see her out there."

"Nope."

I waited.

"What do you mean, nope?"

"Still in th' shed. Have to move them other boats, like I told you."

I broke my cardinal rule and got mad.

"Jesus, Terence, Doug and I have busted our arses to get down here early this morning to get a good start because we have to be back in Toronto Sunday night. We got up before dawn yesterday and drove all day. You promised me you'd have her out and ready so we could hitch up and drive off. Surely it's not too much to ask you to hold up your end of the agreement?"

"Damn boat's not worth all the fuss. Can't drop everthin' else jest like that."

"Well that's just what I'm asking you to do now."

He stalked off toward the upper sheds, muttering to himself.

"He's mean, Dad."

"He's just Terence."

As I was settling my account at the office I could see Terence moving boats around outside with the fork lift. I decided to make things easier for him by backing the trailer, which was still up on the road, down to the parking area. Not a good idea. As I was negotiating the steep curve I swung the wheel the wrong way and jackknifed the trailer hard into the side of the office. Then I couldn't straighten out again and Terence had to come and extricate me.

I was climbing back into the van, still embarrassed, when Terence pointed to the Raven's bow.

"Best take a look at the stem, she's punky right through. Noticed it last fall. Worse now."

It was the area of the bow that had been patched together in St.-Jean and subsequently chewed up on the rocks at Thompson's Point. Major repairs would be required: there would be no question now of putting her in the water until the bow had been reconstructed. Terence looked smug.

"Why thank you for pointing that out, Terence," I said. "No doubt you're happy to be relieved of the awesome responsibility of looking after my balky charge. So now we bid you farewell." I looked him straight in the beady eye and shook his hand. He blinked.

The back wheels of the van spun as we inched up the steep incline with our heavy load. Once we were on level ground the wheels bit and we headed out through Essex and on toward Interstate 87.

"Whew! For a moment I thought I might punch Terence on the nose. Much better to end it on a peaceful note, though."

"I'd've punched him if I was you, Dad."

"I know. Would have been a mistake, though. See, half the reason I felt like punching him was I was so embarrassed about bashing in the office with the trailer. He looked so smug when he came to help me. But if I'd punched him, I wouldn't have felt very good about it after I'd cooled down a bit."

"Dad?"

"Yes, Doug?"

"Did you notice the wheels spinning as we left?"

"I sure did. I was worried we might not make it up that last bit. Hope we don't run into anything like that in the mountains – we don't have four-wheel drive."

"I don't think we'll find anything quite that bad. Driveway was pretty darn steep."

"We'll know soon enough."

At Plattsburgh we stopped to gas up and have lunch. We got out the map and saw that there were several ways we could get to Malone. We chose the one that appeared to be the most direct, Route 374, which heads straight up into the mountains, passing by Lyon Mountain and then skirting the Chateaugay Lakes on the way to Brainardsville. At Brainardsville we could take a secondary road direct to Malone, or continue on Route 374 to the town of Chateaugay and then go west on Route 11 to Malone.

"Don't need to decide which option to take till we get to Brainardsville. We'll ask the locals." I folded the map and paid the bill, using my last U.S. dollars. From now on we would have to use Chargex.

"Dad, don't forget to check the wheel bearings."

"They'll be fine, Doug. If anything was about to go, we'd know about it by now. Remember we've just driven the trailer all the way from Toronto."

All the more reason to check the bearings now, Doug could have answered. But he didn't.

The climb up through the mountains was steep and relentless. The powerful van strained and lurched with its heavy burden, and several times we had to stop to allow it to cool down. We passed through Dannemora and Lyon Mountain and Merrill, then started the slow descent toward Brainardsville.

It was about three in the afternoon when we reached Brainardsville, our needle bouncing on empty. We pulled in to a gas station on the main street. There weren't many people around. It was like a movie set.

"Fillerup?" asked the young attendant.

I showed him my Canadian Chargex card. "You accept this?"

He inspected the card and nodded. His mouth hung open and he didn't seem very bright.

"Okay, then please fill her up and check the oil."

He finished cleaning the windshield. "That'll be $15.77. Oil's fine."

I gave him the Chargex and pulled ahead. A screech of metal on metal came from behind.

"Dad, the wheel's on fire!" Doug was leaning out of the window, looking back. I checked the passenger side mirror and could see smoke billowing from beneath the trailer. We jumped out and ran to the offending wheel. It was obvious the bearing was shot. We stood there wondering what to do.

My shoulder was abruptly nudged and I turned around.

"This yours?"

The speaker was unshaven, dressed in greasy coveralls and an ancient baseball cap. He held a credit card at arm's length, inches from my face, glaring belligerently like a pitcher trying to intimidate the batter.

I backed off to focus on the card. "Yes, that's mine. Why?"

"We don't take no Canadian cards." He drew his lips back over bad teeth as he said the word "Canadian."

"What? That's ridiculous! Your attendant there just told me that my Chargex would be fine. I specifically asked him before we filled up."

"Th'attendant's my son. He don't know nothin'."

"Well then we have a problem, because I don't have any U.S. cash."

"It's your problem, not mine. You Canadians think you can get away with murder, passin' off your cards as if they was worth th' same. Eighty-five cents on the dollar is all she's worth, 'n if you think you can palm it all off on me, you got another think comin'. You can forgit about that, mister."

"Look, number one you get paid fully in American dollars, so you don't need to have any concerns, and number two, as you can see I have a much bigger problem on my hands. This wheel bearing's burned out. I have to get the trailer to somewhere where they can fix it, and now it's 3:30 on a Saturday afternoon, probably not long until closing for the weekend. So I don't have a lot of time to discuss your concerns about my perfectly good Chargex. Please get me pointed in the right direction, and I'll come back as soon as the bearing's fixed. If I can get some cash, you'll get cash, but if not, you'll just have to accept my card."

The son sauntered over to lend filial support. They walked a few paces in front of the van and turned round, arms folded.

"This rig's not leavin' here till I get paid cash in full. Period."

"That's right, mister, cash in full," said the son.

It was a scene right out of *Deliverance*. I could almost hear the duelling banjos. The movie set image intensified until a passing businessman, witness to the impasse, came to the rescue.

"What seems to be the problem?"

"We're from Canada, and this fellow doesn't want to accept my Chargex. We've already filled up with gas and owe him money, but I have no U.S. dollars. Now, to make matters worse, a bearing's shot on the trailer, and we need to get that fixed too. That's going to require more cash. We have to get this all done before closing."

The businessman was friendly and cooperative. "Best thing to do is get yourself to Malone, where there are a number of banks and auto supply places. You'll have to go like hell to beat closing time, but I know for sure Smitty's Auto Supply'll accept your Chargex. You better phone first and find out if they have the part, and ask what time they close."

Smitty's needed the make and model of the trailer in order to identify the bearing, which we were unable to provide as the trailer was unmarked. So now the only way we could establish what kind of bearing we needed was to remove the old one, and for this we needed cash, since the owner wouldn't let us off the property until he was paid. It was Catch-22. I desperately needed a local source of cash.

"Is there a bank in town?"

"Yes, but it's very small and I doubt if they'll give you cash on your Chargex. I'll phone the manager and ask."

The bank manager couldn't help – cashing Chargex was against bank policy.

"I have another idea. Paone's Steak House just down the road may be willing to help. It's four blocks down, this side of the main street. Run down there pronto and I'll phone Franco, the owner. I won't be here when you get back, but good luck!"

We arrived at Paone's completely out of breath. Franco was waiting.

"Marvin tells me you been having trouble with old Art. Poor guy, he's been like that ever since his wife died a few years back. He don't trust anyone now, his own worst enemy. How much cash you need?"

"At least 50 bucks. Seventy-five if you have it."

"Can't handle more than 50, but here's what I'll do. You order a nice meal on the menu here and we'll write it up on your Chargex. Then I'll give you some green stuff and it won't be salad."

It was an elaborate menu for a small town restaurant in the mountains – we could only imagine that it catered to the ski crowd. We picked out the most expensive meal: antipasto, minestrone, smoked salmon, steaks with all the fixings, tiramisu, and Irish coffee. Just ordering it made our mouths water. The bill came to exactly 50 dollars.

"I can't tell you how much we appreciate this, Franco," I said, stuffing the bills in my pocket and backing out. We ran all the way back to the garage.

It was now 4:15 and driving to Malone was out of the question, as Smitty's closed at five. Our only hope was that the small auto supply shop across the street from the garage had the right bearing in stock. Art, the surly garage owner, agreed to pull the defective part now that he knew he'd be paid.

"Need two sets a bearin's, not jest the one. This wheel's near as hot as the one was doin' all the smokin'."

"What time does the auto supply store close?"

"5:00 sharp. Lazy dog, never stays past that on a Saturday. I'll have the first wheel pulled by then, don't you worry. But he won't have the right one in stock anyways. You're gonna have to wait till Monday."

Removing the old bearing was tougher than Art expected. He finally handed me the offending part at 4:55. I ran across the street and entered the shop just as the owner was locking up.

"Boy I'm glad I caught you before you closed. I need two sets of bearings like this." I held out the bearing. "Art over there didn't think you'd have them, said you never carry much stock."

"Art don't know his aunt from a pole in the ground. Let's see that bearing, looks pretty familiar to me. Yeah, sure we got those. You need two sets, you say?"

"You wouldn't believe the hassle I've just gone through. Art wouldn't accept my Chargex because I'm Canadian. Had to go down to Paone's steak house buy a bogus meal just to get cash."

He laughed. "Queer old bugger, that Art, him an' his son Dewey who's not all there. Here, give me your card. I'll charge these up."

By the time we returned Art had pulled the other set of bearings. He packed the new ones with Vaseline from the largest jar of the stuff I had ever seen and reassembled them. Then he pulled the other wheels and repacked their bearings too. He seemed to know what he was doing.

"Vaseline's better'n jest plain grease, cheaper too."

Finally the job was finished and we were ready to set out for Malone. I settled up in cash. Art charged me ten dollars' labour.

"What's the best way to get from here to Malone? Our map shows there's a road that goes direct, but it looks like a back road. Should we continue on 374 to Chateaugay and go the roundabout way?"

"Either way's fine. I take th' direck road meself – bit bumpy but shorter."

We decided to take the direct route and soon regretted it. About five miles along we ran into some major construction and had to take a detour. A mile further the pavement ended, and shortly after that we came to a fork in the road with the detour sign positioned between the two forks, pointing straight ahead.

We took the wrong fork. The road became progressively narrower. Dodging potholes, I desperately looked for a place to turn around. We came to a farm gate to our left. It was just a gate in the fence, no road or drive, but judging by the tractor ruts on either side it had been used regularly. No farmhouse was in sight.

Doug jumped down.

"The gate's locked with a padlock and chain, Dad."

"Try the lock. Sometimes people just leave them closed but not locked."

He gave the thumbs up and swung the gate open. I got out and tested the ground. Despite the deep ruts it seemed firm.

I drove well past the gate and started to back in. To get the trailer headed toward the gate I had to turn the wheel hard to the right, my instincts screaming the opposite. Somehow I managed to get everything more or less in line. Then I gradually swung the wheel to the left in order to keep the van in position as it pushed the trailer through the gate. This was the jacknife stage that had previously defeated me and nearly demolished the marina office.

With Doug's encouragement I slowly inched back. The right wheels of the trailer started to sink under their tremendous load, and soon the rig assumed a precarious angle. I didn't dare stop for fear of getting stuck. The van had good traction on the road surface, and I was getting the knack of keeping the angle right. As the trailer pushed further into the field the left wheels sank too, until the rig was level again.

The moment of truth was at hand. I put the van in drive, crossed my fingers, and to my relief the trailer rolled out again in its own ruts. I pulled out onto the road and waited for Doug to close the gate.

"Tell you one thing, Doug: we're not trying any more detours. We're going back to Brainardsville to take the long way round, no matter how long it takes. No more back roads for us."

Art was just closing up shop as we drove by. He looked at the mud-encrusted trailer and scratched his head.

17

Go-Home

THE RAVEN had been parked in our front driveway for a week and Di was not happy.

"Gordon it's either me or your precious boat. How do you think our neighbours feel about that grotesque monster? Talk about visual pollution! That rusty trailer makes our house look like a junk yard. I mean it: it goes or I go!"

"A little more patience, love, that's all I'm asking. I've arranged to move her this evening after work. Paul Henderson's lending me his van again so I can drive her down to the Toronto Wooden Boatworks."

The Toronto Wooden Boatworks Company Limited was a venture founded by Ulf Hansen and members of the Canadian Shipwright Guild. Located in an old warehouse under the Queen Street Viaduct, its mission was to implement "expert construction, restorations and repairs" on wooden boats.

Ulf carefully examined the Raven from stern to stem. I showed him the replacement section in the transom, and he nodded approvingly: Terence had done a good job despite his hatred of wooden boats. But when we came to the bow, Ulf was horrified.

"What sort of butcher has been at work here?"

"Well actually she broke her mooring last season and took a bit of a superficial abrasion on the . . ."

"No, no, not the scarring on the surface, I mean the repair work. Looks like somebody tried to fix her with a jackhammer and screws and some glue, and now she's all rotten."

I told him about the St.-Jean mishap and the makeshift repairs.

"They should keep people like that under lock and key. She can be fixed, but it's going to take some time and money."

"How much?"

"Leave it with me and I'll work up an estimate."

Ulf called me at the office next morning and we arranged to meet at his shop at noon.

"Here's what we have to do, Mr. Green. We have to pull the motor and turn the boat upside down. Next we have to detach all the planks from the oak stem – that's the part that's riddled with screwholes and is quite rotten. We'll cut the stem back to the sound wood and insert what we call a Dutch Knee."

"Sounds like some kind of birth control device."

He chuckled. "Not exactly. It's just a solid piece of oak, each end bevelled, glued and bolted to the remaining stem. It'll be as strong as the original."

"Is that all?"

"Nearly, but not quite. We have to replace three planks that are too far gone, and also several ribs need reinforcing. Once we've done that, we'll put everything back together and give her a coat of paint. She'll be like new."

"How long is all this going to take?"

"Better part of a month. The total estimate comes to $1,455, and the majority of that is straight labour. The only consolation is you'll have a new boat by the time we've finished."

"Well you better go ahead then – I don't have much option. But I must have her by the middle of June, as we've rented a place in Georgian Bay."

I wondered how I was going to break the news to Di. Perhaps she'd be so relieved the unwelcome driveway occupant had finally left that she'd forget about the cost. That illusion lasted until I got home.

"So you've finally dumped your mistress for a few days. Bet she'll cost you a pretty penny this time."

"Now, Di, you know we had to get her fixed. Actually the cost isn't –"

"I don't even want to hear how much the repairs cost, it'll only make me cross."

🍂 🍂 🍂

Red Rock lay dead ahead. We rounded the marker and headed in toward Go-Home Bay. To our left, behind some islands, lay the Frise cottage; and ahead, not yet visible, would be the Campbell place. The water was rippleless, the early July sky a deep blue.

The Raven was loaded with family, dog and a month's provisions. She ran smoothly, all power and pulsing at my fingertips. I was taking two weeks' vacation at the start of our rental period.

I had phoned John Frise ahead. "So you see, Frisbee, we'll almost be neighbours for the month of July, and you'll have the chance to see the old girl again."

"That's too bad, Gordy, Libby's sister Heather and her husband Nigel are using the place for all of July. You know we own the cottage jointly, and our turn isn't till August. But you'll have to come up later and stay with us. I'll speak to Libs and let you know possible dates."

"That'd be great. Sorry we'll miss you while we're there. But John, since you won't be there to give us advice, is there anything special we should know about Go-Home?"

"Ah, well Gordy, it's . . . it's *Go-Home* – you know, pretty close-knit community, active bush telegraph, especially concerning newcomers. Be sure to stay on the right side of Doris Gibson. She lives on an island near the Campbell place, rules the roost. Good idea to introduce yourself as soon as you arrive."

The entrance to the bay came into view. High on a rock overlooking the entrance was the Campbell cottage. From the water it was just as we had envisaged it: classic 1920s' clapboard architecture, clinging to the rock, leaning away from the prevailing wind to conceal its state of dignified disrepair.

We tied up at the dock and started to unload. Doug and Andy were in a state of high excitement.

"Okay, kids, here's the key. Go on up and open all the doors and windows, air the place out, look it over. Mom and I'll be right up. Take Elly with you."

We finished unloading and were about to head up to the cottage when an outboard pulled up at the dock. The owner, an energetic woman in her fifties dressed in Madras shorts and boating shoes, jumped out and strode toward us, hand extended.

"Welcome to Go-Home. You must be the Greens. Heard you were coming today. I'm Doris Gibson – live on that island over there." She pointed across the bay. We shook hands and introduced ourselves.

"If you need anything, just let me know. I see the Campbells left their outboard out for you, better than the big Raven there for getting about inside the bay, fishing."

"You know the Raven?"

She laughed. "Of course I do. She was here at Go-Home for two years before John sold her to you. I love old boats. Restore them myself for a hobby. Anyway, just popped over to say hello."

"Why thank you, Doris. One thing before we let you go – can you tell us the arrangement for garbage?" Di had been worrying about garbage for days.

"Community collection every Tuesday morning. Just put the garbage bags on the dock and the scow will come by and pick them up."

"That's easy. Well thanks for coming over and making us feel so welcome. I hope we'll see you again soon."

"You will – you can be sure of that. And you'll love it here – it's the purest, most unpolluted place in all of Ontario. We work hard to keep it that way."

It was quite a climb up to the cottage, but the view over the bay was worth it. Andy came running down to meet us.

"Mom, Pop, it's a super place! We've each got a room and I like mine better than Doug's and the kitchen's big and the living room's bigger and there's a huge verandah and the outhouse has a boardwalk and . . ."

The true faded elegance of the Campbell place gradually revealed itself to us. There was no indoor plumbing. An old hand pump by the back door brought water up from the lake, and we had to boil the water for drinking. All the windows had mosquito screens, many of them torn. We had electricity – two of the stove's four elements were working – and the fridge sounded like a walrus with a deviated septum.

That first night tested our mettle. The mosquitoes were at their peak in the hot weather after June's record cold and rain. The high pitched demons competed with the fridge for sonic dominance. By morning we were all badly bitten and exhausted.

I called a family conference.

"Now look, I know this isn't what we were all expecting or what we've been used to. But think of it as camping. It's going to be fun! We'll fix those mosquitoes, don't worry about that. Look how beautiful it is here, how unspoiled! Swimming, fishing, outdoor games, you name it!"

"Forget about the outdoor games," said Di, "First thing we do is clear back the shrubs along the boardwalk to the loo. I can't go there till it's done, it's a snake haven, and I'm bursting." Di has serious snake phobia.

Over the next few days we surrendered to the leisurely rhythms of Go-Home Bay. This was exactly as it was meant to be. Founded in the 1920s by a group of University of Toronto professors, Go-Home has kept itself deliberately remote. The only access is by boat; the closest departure point is Honey Harbour half an hour away. To make a phone call many members still make the boat trip to the solitary public radio phone at the community dock. There is no store. Provisions are ordered by phone or by mail from Gianetto's in Midland and are delivered on the next delivery day along with the mail.

The mosquitoes were a major challenge. We repaired all the screens, but still the critters came down the chimney and through the chinks, attracted at night by the building's residual heat. So we ordered quantities of cheesecloth from Gianetto's and made safari tents and burned coils under the beds. By the third week we had them at bay – more or less.

The boardwalk to the outhouse crossed over a swampy area. We cut back the shrubbery and sprayed to destroy the mosquito larvae, and in so doing disturbed an enormous fox snake that might have escaped from some zoo. It was six feet long and the thickness of my arm. After that, an advance party of beaters was needed each time Di needed to take a pee.

Tuesday was garbage day. We put the bags out on the dock first thing in the morning, glad to be part of a regular collection routine. They were still there that evening.

"Don't worry, Di, I'll stash 'em in the boathouse by the dock till next week. Somebody just forgot to notify the barge people is all. I'll ask Doris what to do next time we see her."

But Doris was away, and the hot weather continued. The garbage turned nasty, a fact that became apparent whenever we were downwind of the boathouse. By the following Tuesday some of the bags had assumed lives of their own. I opened one and was confronted by a seething mass of maggots and an indescribably foul odour. I hastily closed it and set it out for collection on the dock with the other bags.

The garbage scow didn't come that Tuesday either. I returned it to the boathouse, head averted, and latched the door, fearful it might escape. Next afternoon Di opened the door and the fox snake slithered out. That did it.

"Jeedge, that foul mess goes. Now!"

"Whoa, love, listen! We can't bury it in the rock, can we? And we daren't burn it because the bush is tinder dry. What do you suggest we should do?"

"Deep six it."

"Hmmm, not a bad idea, if we can find a place deep enough."

We got out the chart. The waters of Go-Home Bay are generally shallow, but there are a couple of deeper spots. One of these is a 40-foot deep trench a quarter of a mile off the Campbell cottage, toward Doris Gibson's island.

"We sink the garbage there, the natural forces of nature take over. Fish will eat the maggots, slowly return to the food chain. Too deep for any currents to bother anybody. Just this once, mind you. Wouldn't want to make a habit of it. Only in an emergency like this."

At dusk I quietly lugged the five offending bags down to the beach and filled them with large stones, double-bagging them and sealing them tightly. Then with muffled oars I rowed out in the aluminum boat. I didn't dare use the outboard.

When I judged I was over the deepest part, I dumped the whole mess over the side. The stones made a dreadful clatter against the aluminum, and within seconds lights went on at the Gibson dock and an outboard headed out. Then I saw to my horror that not one of the bags had sunk. The tightly sealed outer bags acted as flotation bladders.

"What seems to be the problem?" asked Doris.

I was surrounded by floating garbage bags. The evidence was so overwhelming I simply shrugged and started loading the bags back in the boat.

"Scum!" she hissed.

I winced.

"Filthy scum! Think they can use our pristine wilderness as a garbage dump! Gordon I'm so glad you noticed this outrage and came to pick up the mess. You've entered into the true spirit of Go-Home."

"Er, Doris . . ."

"Yes?"

"There's something I must . . . well . . . these aren't somebody else's garbage bags, they're ours."

George Washington could not have put it better.

"What?" she spluttered, "you mean you . . . good lord, man, don't you realize we all take our drinking water straight from the lake? What sort of madness is this?"

I explained the collection mixup, how we had tried unsuccessfully to contact her, and how finally in desperation we had got out the charts and decided to sink the garbage in the deepest part of the bay.

"So that's how it is, Doris. I can't say I feel very good about this." In reality I felt about two inches tall.

"Well you certainly didn't use your head, but you're new here and deserve the benefit of the doubt. Here's what I'll do. Take this flashlight – I know these waters well, and don't need it. I'll lead you into the bay to Go-Home River and point you in the direction of the garbage dump which is about a mile up the river. From there you're on your own. Please return the flashlight in the morning."

I tried to memorize landmarks as we headed across the bay in the gloaming. We came to the mouth of the river and Doris circled, pointing in the direction of the dump, then took off. I sat there as the sound of her engine faded into silence.

On the trip up the river I could see the general outline of the shore, but the surface of the water was visible only a few yards ahead, so I had to go dead slow. The air was thick with mosquitoes and other denizens of the swampy area. I pulled my shirt over my head and peeped through the collar hole, exposing my back.

Beating the air, I scrambled onto the garbage dock and dumped the unwholesome mess into a container, then fled back to the boat and down the river as fast as I dared. Once out on the bay I opened the little outboard wide and let the cooling breeze blow the mosquitoes away. There was still just enough light to pick out the landmarks.

Di ran down to the dock.

"Oh Jeedge I saw the whole thing. Was she really angry?"

"She was absolutely furious at first. Then I explained our predicament and she became quite understanding. She even lent me her flashlight. But I was humiliated, Di, I tell you. I'll never, ever, try to deep six a garbage bag again."

৩ ৩ ৩

The run-in with Doris Gibson marked a watershed in our stay at Go-Home. After that we adjusted to the leisurely pace of island living. We spent as much time on the water as off, and in the long soft evenings we idled and read, even dabbled in painting. Too soon our month came to an end.

ॐ ॐ ॐ

That August we returned to Go-Home to visit John and Libby Frise. John was waiting on the dock, pantomiming. He made an exaggerated megaphone with his hands.

"Oh Libby," he called up to the cottage, "here comes the garbage scow now. Last call for any junk."

The story of our shame had preceded us. That weekend John showed no mercy. He used every imaginable excuse to bring up the subject of garbage. He didn't realize that he would soon become the butt of an even larger joke, one which would become a Go-Home legend.

But he did enthuse over the Raven. She looked immaculate in her varnished brightwork and new coat of paint. At my request he showed me over his Windy 22, all gleaming white fibreglass, but he kept looking over his shoulder at the Raven.

"Want to go for a spin in the old girl?"

"What are we waiting for?"

We climbed in the Raven and headed out to Red Rock.

"She's all yours, Frisbee," I said, stepping back and making a small bow in the direction of the wheel.

He braced himself against the wheel, silver hair streaming, a broad smile on his mobile features.

"No more spoke in your fly," I shouted.

"How so?"

"Fixed her. Small piece of metal over the rudder did the trick. Go ahead, try her."

He opened the throttle full and carved a turn to starboard, then swung her hard in the opposite direction, completing the manoeuvres with a series of tight dipsy-doodles.

"Ah Green, she is a magnificent craft, magnificent! She never handled like this before. How on earth did you manage it?"

"That small piece of metal is all. Century Boat Works told me how to do it."

I thought I detected a subtle change in the engine note – more like a purr than a snarl. But John's hand wasn't even near the throttle.

18

The Wreck of the Windy

THE TRANQUILLITY of our Go-Home experience did little to convince us that island living was for us. Transferring bags and groceries in and out of boats quickly palled: we preferred the convenience of being able to drive to and from the cottage at will. So the following year we rented a rambling old cottage on a sandy beach a couple of miles east of Penetanguishene.

The beach was sheltered by a headland to the west and by Beausoleil Island to the north, so it was safe to put out a mooring for the Raven. Fearful of a repeat of the Thompson's Point experience, I anchored the mooring entirely by heavy duty chain to a truck engine block in 15 feet of water. Whenever we were away we kept the boat at Dutchman's Cove Marina.

Bill Van Rijn, the owner of Dutchman's Cove, was delighted to see us back. He rubbed his hands as we discussed necessary repairs. The Raven had started to leak again, and her engine was wheezing bronchially.

"Those twin carburettors are really finicky. The mechanic's adjusted them best he can, but he says you need a complete rebuild. Also a couple of valves are stuck."

"How much is that going to set me back?"

"Couple hundred for the carburettors. Valves could be quite a bit more if we have to take the heads off."

"What about the leaking?"

"Bottom of the transom's punky, right below the new plank."

"Can you patch it for the rest of the season?"

"That's what I was going to suggest. She'll still leak a bit, but you can get by until the fall. Then we'll do the major overhaul." He rubbed his hands again. "Have to get those valves unstuck, though."

We kept the Raven at her mooring despite the leaking. The twin float switches for the pump functioned flawlessly, too well in fact, for the pump had a habit of cutting in at the quietest moments. One night our neighbours woke up to the sound of a moose urinating in the water. They crept outside, armed with binoculars and a flash camera, and surprised the Raven relieving herself *in flagrante delicto*.

ॐ ॐ ॐ

One September Saturday back in Toronto I ran into Libby Frise at the local market.

"Hi, Libs, haven't seen you in ages. How was the summer at Go-Home?"

"You mean John hasn't told you?"

"No, we haven't talked in quite a while."

"Well I'm not surprised he hasn't called you. Poor old John's taken an awful ribbing."

"Why? What happened?"

Libby's was an incredible story. On the afternoon of Friday, July 30, 1982, she and the two girls were all packed and ready to leave for their month's stay at Go-Home. John had taken the afternoon off to attend part of the second day's play at the Canadian Open golf tournament at Glen Abbey. He was now very late.

When he got home it was nearly dark. The family was hungry and cross, so they had to stop for hamburgers on the way. They didn't reach Honey Harbour until after 11:00 P.M. Loading the boat took more time, for Libby had packed a month's supply of groceries and a quantity of fresh fruit for conserving including two dozen baskets of raspberries.

Finally the boat was loaded and the passengers embarked. These included John, Libby, Heather and Gillian, Libby's two Siamese cats, Gillian's pet rabbit Clover, and of course Tramp, Wild Dog of the North.

The warm night embraced them. There was no moon, but the heavens danced so brightly they felt they could reach out and touch the stars. John could just make out the familiar outlines of islands flying by.

They negotiated the channel around the north end of Beausoleil Island without difficulty and headed across the open water toward Whelan's.

"Gillian, here's the spotlight. Train it on that marker to the right, will you? That's where we make our turn."

"What marker, Dad? I can't see any marker."

"Right there," he said, pointing into the dark.

"I still can't see it, Dad."

"Oh here, give me that spotli –"

The heavens exploded. Glass pounded on rock and rock launched them on a trajectory to the stars. They hung there for a moment before coming down with a vicious jolt and the deafening scream of tortured metal. Crashing bushes, the keel rocking on bedrock, then silence.

Libby looked up into branches. Pine needles stood out against the brilliant night sky. John traced the spotlight over pandemonium. Grocery bags had burst over the floor and raspberries were scattered everywhere. Gillian was sobbing.

"Clover, I can't find Clover. Oh, Dad, where's Clover?"

"Forget about your rabbit. What about my boat?"

They were fortunate. They had hit a gently sloping rock at just the right angle and had been launched like a ski jumper high into the bushes. Had the rock been sharp the story would have been very different.

No one was hurt, not even Clover. As they sat there wondering what to do next, they heard an outboard.

The boat's lights appeared and they all started yelling, but it just kept going. John took the Windy's spotlight and swung it wildly above his head. This caught the driver's attention and he veered toward them. He came close and slowed, his face caught in the glare of the spotlight. He was looking up, mouth agape.

"Up here! We're up here!"

"Jesus! Who's up where? What's up there? Can't see with that light in my eyes. Jesus."

"Sorry."

John swept the spotlight over the bushes and the Windy, then down to the water's edge. The man beached his boat.

"Jesus!"

His limited vocabulary made conversation difficult, but he finally recovered his faculties and agreed to take John and Heather to the Frise cottage where John would pick up his own outboard and come back for Libby and Gillian and the pets and provisions. They would deal with the Windy in the morning. It was only then that Libby saw that the man had a baby in the boat.

Libby and Gillian watched the outboard's lights disappear into the night. They felt alone with the stars. The whine of the motor grew fainter.

WHAM! Bambity-bambity-screee-eee-unch!

Lights popped on all around the outboard. Poor Good Samaritan! He had met the same fate as the Windy, right in the middle of a group of populated islands.

Georgian Bay islanders are a close breed, and when one of their own is in distress they rally to the cause. In no time at all two boats were launched to take the shipwrecked mariners home. At John's insistence all were sworn to secrecy. They could readily appreciate John's embarrassment: boating accidents, particularly avoidable ones caused by carelessness or stupidity, are severely frowned upon.

It was after four in the morning when they wearily lugged the last load of provisions up to the cottage.

"Libs, you and the girls go off to bed. I'm heading back to Honey Harbour to find Greg at the marina. Any luck we'll have the Windy pulled off the rocks and towed away before anyone's awake."

⚓ ⚓ ⚓

Dawn's rosy fingers caressed the sky as John rounded the marker off Red Rock. Twenty minutes later he passed the infamous launchpad. The sun was up now, and he could see the Windy peeping through the bushes, her transom glinting in the sun's reflected rays. He marvelled at how far off course he had been.

⚓ ⚓ ⚓

Greg was already up, sitting in his kitchen.

"Greg? It's John Frise."

"Who? Oh, John, come on in. You're up bright and early. What's up?"

"I have a real emergency. Boat's on the rocks and I need to get her off before anyone sees her. Can you help?"

Greg loved emergencies, particularly where the dignity of one of his customers was at stake. Within minutes he had enlisted two helpers and had drawn up a list of the equipment they would need. By 6:30 a.m. the crew had gathered aboard the marina's large aluminum work boat, armed with tow ropes, jacks, a come-along, inflatable rollers, and an axe to clear the bushes. By 6:50 A.M. they were at the crash site.

To John's relief Greg didn't waste time marvelling over the position of the Windy or the circumstances of the mishap.

"Outdrive leg's completely ruined. Gotta take the lower portion off anyway or we'll never drag her back. She'll float, though. No holes in the hull."

With quiet efficiency they cleared the bushes, unbolted and removed the outdrive, and jacked up the transom to put rollers under the keel. They fastened a long line to the bow and made two turns around a nearby tree to act as a brake. A slipway was made with more rollers to the water's edge. When everything was set, Greg rowed out in the dinghy and dropped the Windy's anchor.

The anchor line was attached to the come-along which in turn was attached to the Windy's stern. They started to winch back on the come-along. Inch by inch, then foot by foot, the Windy retraced her path. By 7:30 she was being towed back to Honey Harbour.

❧ ❧ ❧

John was elated. He wasn't even tired. The sun reflected warmly off Red Rock and the wind blew in his silver hair. Nobody had witnessed his humiliation, and now he was almost home and the Windy was safely squirrelled away. By the time word got out, as it surely would, she would be back in the water and the incident would be just one more boating mishap.

He tied up at the dock and climbed up to the cottage. Libby and the girls were already up. He had forgotten that this was the weekend of the Go-Home Bay Regatta. The girls were entered in several of the events.

"How'd it go, John?"

"Ah, Libs, that Greg is so fast and efficient. Got us off the rocks in no time. Discreet, too, no embarrassing questions. I know he and his crew won't say a word – they promised that. But I'm worried about you and the girls, to be perfectly honest. You're likely to blab something during the Regatta. It's not just me, you know, it's the other fellow as well. I can't tell you how embarrassing it would be for both of us if word got out of our separate accidents."

"Aw come on, Dad, we know the score," said Heather.

"Good. Well I'm going to bed, get myself rested up for the big party tonight."

Libby, Heather and Gillian went off tight-lipped to the Regatta. Not a question was asked nor a word spoken.

ॐ ॐ ॐ

That night was the Regatta Party – the big social event of the summer. As they tied up the outboard at the community dock John once more admonished the family of the importance of loyalty and silence.

Libby saw some friends on the dock and went over to talk to them. By the time she got to the party John was already surrounded by a crowd. His hands were doing all the talking. He pointed up to the sky, shaded his eyes with his hand, swept a light down at his feet, rocked a baby in his arms.

Libby couldn't believe her eyes or her ears. John the raconteur simply couldn't hold back. He had to tell anyone and everyone who would listen the story of his shame and deliverance. As you might expect, the accident lost nothing in the telling: no detail was spared or diminished. Gone were his concerns for himself and the other boater. With reckless abandon he sealed his own fate, made his own legend, established forever his rightful place in the lore of Go-Home Bay.

ॐ ॐ ॐ

After hearing Libby's story I called John. I wanted to hear the whole grisly tale from the other horse's mouth. John said he had an idea that might be of interest, so we arranged lunch.

"Libby told me the whole thing, John. I guess you should thank your lucky stars that no one was hurt and the Windy's hull was undamaged."

"Aah, Gordy . . ."

He sighed, eased his collar, looked over his shoulder, leant over the table.

"It's – it's the humiliation of it all!" he whispered through taught lips. "Half of Go-Home was there at the party, for godsakes, and I had to go and blather it all over the place! I may never live this down."

"Oh, come on, Frisbee, it's not that bad. A few months from now everyone will have forgotten all about it. Look at it this way: you get a brand new outdrive and prop from the insurance, and the boat's as good as new."

"That's what I wanted to talk to you about. I've always thought the Windy was a tad underpowered. Now I'm thinking of putting the insurance proceeds toward a new Volvo unit to replace the Mercruiser 185 – more powerful and much more efficient."

"That's interesting, but where do I come in?"

"I thought you might be interested in buying the Mercruiser. The engine itself is perfectly good – only the outdrive was demolished."

Now he really had my attention. The Raven's Interceptor was burning oil and a major repair bill was looming. I was intrigued at the prospect of stepping up from the old Interceptor to a more powerful and modern Mercruiser.

"Wonder if it would fit the Raven? It's an inboard/outboard, not a straight inboard like the Interceptor."

"I know, but both engines are built on a Ford block, so it might work. With any luck the Mercruiser would hook right up with the Raven's Borg Warner transmission."

"Sounds logical. Tell you what, John: if it fits, you have yourself a deal."

꒳ ꒳ ꒳

That winter the Raven went through a major transformation. I didn't like to discuss the cost, but my secretiveness with the family only fanned the flames. For Christmas I received two plaques. The first was a discreet brass one to be mounted on the boat's dash. It read:

> **This boat was once part of the Swiss Navy. That's why there are so many holes in it.**

The second plaque was the more familiar definition of "boat," mounted on oiled walnut, to be hung on my study wall:

> **Boat (bot) n. A hole in the water, surrounded by wood, into which one pours money.**

It was bitterly cold. High snowbanks bordered Highway 93 on the approach to Penetang and the harbour was completely frozen over.

"Mr. Green, as you can see we've replaced the rotten transom. We'll stain and varnish it as soon as the warmer weather comes, but I want to point out something else on the deck." Bill rubbed his hands together briskly. "We've found a bit of leaking around the hatch. I recommend you rip off that old painted canvas and let the wood breathe. Restore her to her original mahogany pinstripe – she'll look far more classy."

Bill knew his customer. I protested that his suggestion was impractical because the varnish would deteriorate in the sun's rays, but he had a simple answer for that: a vinyl halter-top that could easily be removed and replaced each time we went out. He had reached my soft underbelly. Anything to make the Raven look more classy.

"Okay, Bill, you go ahead with that, but what about the new motor?"

"Mechanic's had a heck of a time. Everything fit perfectly, then he discovered that the Mercruiser turns in the opposite direction to the old Interceptor."

"In the opposite direction? How's that possible?"

"Beats me. For a while there we thought you'd have to buy a new transmission. I held off phoning you because I didn't think you'd appreciate hearing what that was going to cost. Anyway, the mechanic phoned Borg Warner and they told him just to hook the old transmission up backwards! Can you believe that? Now all you need is a new prop with the opposite pitch."

᠊ᢣ ᢣ ᢣ

I waited anxiously for the warm weather so I could try out the Raven with her new heart and external finery. Bill phoned in mid June.

"She's in the water, all set to go, tight as a barrel, no leaking at all. Slight list to starboard with the new motor is all. She looks great."

᠊ᢣ ᢣ ᢣ

Bill proudly led me down to the docks. The Raven bobbed jauntily, her burnished mahogany deck aglow, precise white pinstripes detailing the entire topsides. She looked fantastic, except for that ridiculous hatch cover. Previously the off-white colour of the toilet seat had blended with the painted canvas of the foredeck; now it stood out like rude graffiti against a dignified antique.

"Bill, that hatch looks ridiculous. At least paint it a mahogany colour so it won't stand out like a sore thumb."

"Good idea. Never thought of that."

I lifted the engine box. The mechanic had done a professional job with new control connections and electrical paraphernalia. Everything was squeaky clean. When I started the new engine I noted with delight that it still had the old familiar snarl. Bill untied the lines and pushed me out.

I headed for the middle of the harbour and gradually opened her up. As I did so she listed to starboard. The faster I went, the more she went over. I didn't dare run her full open for fear I would spill out.

I went back to the dock.

"Bill, there's something seriously wrong. She wants to travel on her side."

"I know, I could see that. It's worse than I realized."

"Well what can you do about it?"

He took a deep breath.

"Here's the situation, Mr. Green. All inboards are designed with the shaft slightly off centre to compensate for the torque of the turning propellor. Your boat was built for the Interceptor which turned one way. The new Mercruiser turns the opposite way. I think you can see what I mean."

The horrible reality sank in.

"You mean there's nothing we can do? Why didn't you tell me this before?"

"To be honest we didn't think of it until we tried her out."

"Can't we just move the shaft?"

"No, not without taking out a section of the keel. I wouldn't recommend that."

"Jesus, Bill, what do you suggest, then? You don't seriously expect me to drive her as she is, do you?"

"No way, not now I've seen how badly she keels over. But I'm sure a set of trim tabs will do the trick. We can install some good electrical ones, that way you can keep the boat level with a flip of the switch no matter how many people are on board or how fast you're going." He brought his hands half way together and dropped them with an embarrassed grin.

༉ ༉ ༉

We rented the same cottage on the beach east of Penetang for the next three summers. The Raven with her gleaming decks and incongruous trim tabs became part of the community. We ranged ever farther afield: soon all of the islands south of O'Donnell Point were familiar territory.

One of our favourite islands was South East Wooded Pine. This five-acre piece of sculptured pink and grey granite, topped by contorted old white pines and surrounded by sparkling, clear blue-green waters and shallow reefs, has a natural harbour at the north end and good anchorage on the leeward side. The owner, Miss Robinson of Go-Home Bay, didn't mind picnickers landing for the day. A sign posted near the anchorage told everybody as much:

NOTICE TO CAMPERS
Please treat this island as your own.
Clean up garbage.
Put out all fires.
Don't feed the rattlesnakes.

In reality there were plenty of rattlesnakes on South East Wooded Pine but we seldom encountered them. We were more interested in the other wildlife. Each summer hundreds of migratory terns arrived to nest, and the island was sanctuary to gulls and other species as well. The shoals around the island provided shelter for smallmouth bass and crayfish, and the clear waters afforded excellent snorkelling. One of my favourite tricks was to dive down about 15 feet and pick up two rocks. The rocks provided negative buoyancy and enabled me to stay down without kicking. I would knock the rocks together and wait. Soon the inquisitive bass would come out of their crevices to investigate. Often they would nibble at my face mask.

꙳ ꙳ ꙳

Georgian Bay became such an integral part of our lives that we yearned to own property there again. We contacted Bryson McQuirter, the local realtor, and did the rounds of properties for sale. But prices had soared, and I wasn't sure we'd ever be able to afford it. Still we looked, if only to crystallize our likes and dislikes.

Then in the summer of 1984 Di was diagnosed with a serious form of cancer. After surgery to remove the tumour the outlook was bleak, and I was devastated beyond belief. But friends and family rallied round, and that wonderful person incredibly pulled through all the treatments, thanks largely to her plucky mental attitude. In the process, my own perspectives changed forever.

19

Toanche

WHAT POINT WAS THERE in saving for a rainy day if that rainy day might then elude us? I was determined to find a Georgian Bay property. Theoretically we still couldn't afford a second home, but DS was setting record profits and my own contribution to the firm was well recognized. The future looked bright. My bank manager agreed.

We had a clear idea of what we wanted. Western exposure, close to Penetang, the cottage itself bright and attractive, well sited, and in good repair. There should be good swimming and definitely somewhere to keep the boat.

Armed with a potential bankroll, we inspected close to 50 properties that summer. None came close to matching our criteria. On the last weekend, as we were packing our belongings into the car, Bryson McQuirter phoned.

"Gordon? There's a property that's about to be listed that I think you should see. I'll be right over."

Bryson drove us through Penetang and across the entire peninsula to Nottawasaga Bay, about a 20-minute drive. Then he headed north to a point opposite Christian Island.

"Where are you taking us, Bryson? This is much farther from Penetang than we've considered."

"Just wait."

"But you can't moor a boat on this shore, that's why we haven't even looked."

"I know, but just wait, you'll see."

Di liked the property immediately. Her practised eye saw through the common brown exterior and small windows, focussed on the architectural layout.

"Jeedge, a little bit of cosmetics and it's perfect. Get rid of the poky windows and green shag rug, open the place up, put in sliding glass doors and skylights, it'll be fabulous. Four bedrooms, den, two fireplaces, front and back decks, basement, gorgeous property, what more do we need? Look at the view. Imagine the sunsets!"

ᕁ ᕁ ᕁ

We called it Toanche (Toe-WAN-chay) after the Huron village of that name. Thrice sacked by the Iroquois and twice moved, Toanche's final location is believed to have been somewhere on the peninsula west of Penetanguishene. Toanche is an Algonquian word meaning "place of embarkation" - fitting name for a place that launched a new phase in our lives.

Toanche faced west, its view framed by nearby Christian Island to the north and the Blue Mountains of Collingwood to the southwest. Straight across Nottawasaga Bay the distinctive headland of Cape Rich projected clearly above the horizon, marking the entrance to Owen Sound, a deep inlet whose namesake town, more than 40 miles distant, glowed in the night sky. North of Owen Sound, over the horizon, spread the invisible finger of the Bruce Peninsula separating Georgian Bay from Lake Huron.

The sunsets were always on the march. In spring the sun moved ever northward until by mid-June it descended like a molten cannonball right on top of Christian Island. By mid-winter it had moved far south, almost to the Blue Mountains. The summer sunsets glowed crimson on the granite boulders lining Toanche's foreshore; those in winter sparkled pink off the ice and snow.

From water's edge the sand disappeared to eternity. The swimming was like the ocean, only the blue-green water was sweet and clear. When the west wind blew, breakers crashed onto the rocky shore and sifted back over the sand, providing body surfing by day and soothing white sound by night.

The cottage itself sat well back, partially protected from the prevailing wind. No one put out a mooring on this exposed shore, and few even ventured to build a dock. This was distressing to me, and I demurred; yet when I saw the hurt in Di's eyes and realized how much this decision meant to her, I quickly changed my mind. It was the best decision I ever made.

꒜ ꒜ ꒜

Sunday, October 27, 1985, my birthday. I was alone with Eloise, driving up Highway 93 on my way to inspect the new pine floor and windows that had been installed that week. There was also a small marina nearby I wished to look into for possible boat storage and berthing.

Just after Wyebridge I turned onto an unpaved concession road, short cut to Perkinsfield. A siren sounded and I pulled over. The officer was agitated.

"Thought you could make a run for it, did you?"

"No, officer, I had no idea you were there. I'm just taking the short cut to Perkinsfield. Have I done something wrong? I'm sure I wasn't speeding."

"Going into the school zone I clocked you at . . . aaargh! Phtt!"

Eloise stuck her head out of the window and gave his moustache a slurping wet lick.

"Eloise, back off! I'm sorry, officer. Did you say school zone?"

"Yes, sir, I was driving towards you, and clocked you at 50 kilometres entering the school zone. When you saw me you turned off onto this concession."

"Officer, I repeat I never saw you and I'm afraid I never saw the school zone either."

"Well, sir, you did pull over promptly when I gave you the siren, I'll grant you that much. But I'm going to have to . . . aaargh!"

Elly's timing was perfect. When I finally managed to pull the dog back into the car the poor man's shoulders were shaking. Not with rage, but with laughter.

"Officer, it's my birthday and a very special day. I'm on my way to visit our new cottage, and I don't yet know the road well. Please don't wreck my day."

The policeman took off his dark glasses and wiped them, then dabbed his eyes. He must have had a soft spot for dogs, for he leant over and looked kindly through the window, then lowered his voice.

"You'd better get yourself and that attack dog out of here fast, sir, before I book you for keeping a dangerous assault animal. Don't ever let me catch you speeding in that school zone again. Oh, and happy birthday."

That encounter set the tone for the morning. The renovations had transformed a humdrum frame dwelling into a place of airiness and light. I made some mental notes about landscaping and left to find the marina.

༉ ༉ ༉

Albert's Cove Marina is tucked behind a point of land on the 17th Concession. Battered by the prevailing wind, it ekes out a precarious existence behind a tenuous breakwater of boulders providing protection for 50 or so boats.

Hubert Charlebois lived on the property. He was operating a large mechanical shovel on top of the breakwater as I drove in. (The shovel, which could be seen for miles around, was a recognizable landmark to boaters. During high water years, such as 1986, it was in constant use.) Hubert shut down the machine and removed his hearing protectors.

"No, we don't have any space next season, and there's a waiting list. But a wooden boat, you say? Don't have much truck with wooden boats – had too many bad experiences."

"Not another Terence," I muttered.

"What's that?"

"I said what a lovely terrace! I was just admiring the view from your house."

"Why thank you. Yes, I just finished laying the paving stones this morning. Grass goes in tomorrow. But with regard to your boat, I'll put your name on the waiting list. Check back in the spring."

This was disappointing. The 15-mile trip to Penetang each time we wished to take the boat out would be a drag. I vowed to persuade

Hubert to make room in the spring. Now I thought about it, he really seemed like quite a decent fellow, not at all like Terence. Perhaps a little seasonal cheer at Christmas would help expand his docking capacity.

⚓ ⚓ ⚓

As soon as the renovations were finished we started to drive up on weekends. The luxury of owning a fully winterized cottage was a new experience. Bitter wind blew off the frozen bay and drove the snow in deep drifts. Twice we had to dig our way in on arrival. Yet always it was warm inside.

Lafontaine, closest village to Toanche, hosted "Lafontaine en Action," a popular cross-country ski centre, and the surrounding provincial forest was interlaced with snowmobile trails. Sometimes we would drive to Lafontaine to ski, but often we would take off directly from our front door, skiing through the hardwood forest and scaling the 200-foot bluff that parallels the shore. Afterwards we would stoke up the wood-burning sauna and thrash each other with aromatic old birch leaves. Then I would roll in the snow and yelp like a crazed Finn.

In March the days grew longer and the sap flowed. We found a sugar maple operation not a mile from the cottage. The syrup was sweet and tasty.

On May 3 the first hummingbird arrived.

⚓ ⚓ ⚓

The Christmas spirit had definitely warmed Hubert Charlebois, but not enough to persuade him to make room for the Raven. We had no choice but to keep the boat another year at Dutchman's Cove. Bill called cheerfully in mid-June to advise that he had launched her and she was leaking badly.

"Good grief, Bill, not again! Are you sure she's had enough time in the slings? Don't do any major repairs until I see for myself."

I went up the following weekend.

"As you can see, Mr. Green, we've tightened the screws best we can, and used lots of that black goop. That's stopped the leaking for now. But the planks have separated again in the same place where she was badly stored that first winter. She needs a couple false ribs there, and two new planks."

"Can't we get by for the summer this way?"

"Don't recommend it. But you're the boss."

"Well I'm not in a spending mood. Better give me a supply of spare screws and some more of that black goop." The cottage renovations had set me back plenty. Bill looked dejected.

⚓ ⚓ ⚓

Our first guests at Toanche were the Crosbies. Allan, a former Harvard classmate, ran his own successful merchant banking firm in Toronto. He had met Missy, a North Carolinian of great charm, intelligence and determination, while at Harvard, and they married shortly after Allan's graduation. They now had three sons.

Allan's wavy fair hair and fresh complexion reminded one of the kid next door. His manner of speech did little to dispel that notion, for his mind was always ten sentences ahead of what he was trying to say. A superb writer and thinker with a masters degree in Economics from Oxford University as well as a Harvard MBA, his sentences would begin: "Uh, gee, d'you think . . . well, what I mean is . . ."

We finished breakfast on the patio and were discussing the day's boating plans. It was a warm July day, not a cloud in the sky.

Di argued for a change in picnic venue. "We don't always have to go to the Pine Islands or Giant's Tomb, you know. We haven't even tried Christian Island yet, let alone Hope or Beckwith, and they're much closer now that we're on this shore."

"I know, Di, but Beckwith's crowded on weekends, and there aren't many beaches on Christian. Let's try Hope – I've noticed a beach there at the south end."

Allan and I drove to Penetang to fetch the Raven while the girls prepared the picnic. We took along a supply of beer for the trip back.

The run by water from Penetang to the cottage normally took about 40 minutes. A gentle breeze ruffled the surface as we passed Gin Rocks and changed course toward the south end of Giant's Tomb. It was a perfect day for boating.

"Hey, Gordon, this is . . . aah . . . it's just . . . uh, hey, want a beer?"

We opened a can of Heineken and the breeze blew in our hair and the Raven purred. Ahead lay the gap between Beckwith and the mainland, and beyond that Christian Island. As we neared Beckwith the engine note changed. The Raven was straining and I wasn't sure why.

Water came over the floorboards. I cut the engine, and a massive volume of water poured in. I checked over the side and saw a plank hanging loose below the waterline – one of the planks Bill had tried to repair. We were sinking fast, a mile off shore.

Without a second's hesitation I threw off my clothes, grabbed some rags and dove over the side. I stuffed the rags into the hole and temporarily stanched the leaking. The bilge pump still ran full tilt.

Crosbie was peering over the side. "Gee, Gordon, d'you do this . . . I mean, is this something that . . ."

I backed away, treading water.

"No problem, Crosberry, we just popped a plank is all. We'll let her pump a few minutes then I'll screw the plank back in place." Just an ordinary occurrence. Happens every day.

I always kept mask, snorkel and flippers on the boat. Hastily donning them I slid back into the water to inspect the damage. It looked to be a straightforward temporary repair job – the screws had torn away from the ribs, so a few strategically placed longer screws should hold the plank in place until the ribs could be replaced.

Allan had lost interest and was buried in the pages of the *Economist*. He absent-mindedly handed tools over the side as I called for them. Armed with black goop, a handful of screws and the screwdriver, I sank silently beneath the surface and plucked out the rags. The water rushed in. Working quickly, I slathered the sticky compound around the overlapping edges and turned my attention to the first screw.

I couldn't gain any purchase. There was nothing to hold on to, and when I pushed on the screw I glided gently away from the boat. I couldn't for the life of me think of what I could use to steady myself. Heart pounding, I regrouped. A more direct frontal assault was called for. Gathering myself like a jousting knight I charged the screw, screwdriver at the ready and flippers thrashing. Twice I overshot the target and wound up embracing the goop-covered hull. On my third try I made contact with the screw and gave it a quick half turn before shooting back like a pinball. With this tenuous toe-hold I redoubled my efforts. Progress was agonizingly slow. I still kept missing and smearing more black goop all over myself. By the time I finished I was exhausted and a complete mess.

I flopped back into the boat and lurched against the rail, Horatio at the bridge, heroic and naked and shivering and smothered in greasepaint. Raising my head to acknowledge the expected hero's welcome I saw to my utter disbelief that Allan was totally oblivious, still engrossed in the *Economist*. The man had no appreciation of the agony

I had just endured nor any idea of how close we had come to a grim assignation with King Neptune. Outraged, I gave a noisy huff through my snorkel. He looked up and blinked twice. "Gosh, Gordon, I never knew . . . I mean . . ." He looked more closely at my face, then reached into the cooler. "Uh, here, Mammy, want another beer?"

20

Parting

NINETEEN EIGHTY-SIX was the year John Frise died from complications following open heart surgery – his second operation in less than five years. The knife-edge tensions of the risk arbitrage business finally took their toll.

John's premature death was a dreadful shock to us all and brought us face to face with our own mortality. At the reception following his funeral a number of us vowed not to let this singular character's memory quickly die. So was born the John Frise Dinner, an annual gathering of Frise's friends and admirers at which this unique Canadian's exploits were remembered, embellished and immortalized. The event, which was continued for several years, was always held at The Toronto Golf

Club, that venerable establishment rich in tradition where John himself had been a proud member.

᭡ ᭡ ᭡

I can't explain why, but with John died my obsession over the Raven. Possibly our three lives had been so interwoven that when one leg fell off the stool, the whole thing toppled. The Raven, for her part, never let me forget what a low form of life I was for abandoning her in my affections. Each trip we made to and from Penetang, each visit to the marina, gave her fresh opportunity to dramatize her ailments. And with each incident I saw her more clearly through Di's eyes.

That summer I worked on a major initial public share offering for a Newfoundland fish products company. During a lull between due diligence sessions in St. John's I visited a boating supply store where I found a box compass, a precisely engineered instrument to be used by fishermen in the foggy inshore waters, designed to be removed from the dory at the end of the day's fishing. This beautiful and practical piece seemed ideal. As long as I had the Raven, I could lock it in the cabin at the end of the day's boating, away from thieving eyes at the marina. And if the Raven and I eventually parted, I could take the compass with me.

I read up on installing or "swinging" a marine compass. It is not an easy matter. One has to take the boat out onto open water, clear of magnetic interference, and orient her along several known bearings to compare the compass reading with the actual bearing and adjust for magnetic distortion from the engine and instrument panel. Flat calm conditions are required, a rare event in Georgian Bay. It took numerous tries and adjustments on three separate occasions before I was satisfied I had oriented the frame (into which I would fit the removable compass box) correctly. Now I was anxious to prove the compass's worth.

We were invited that weekend to visit Liz and Jim Meekison at their island far up the bay, a good piece north of Parry Sound. Normally we would have gone by car, but I wanted to test the new compass and my navigational prowess. The distance was 60 miles as the crow flies across open water. It was more than double that distance if one drove.

"Green, be serious," said Di. "You're nuts if you think I'd even remotely contemplate crossing the middle of Georgian Bay in that leaky old tub. What if she pops another plank? You won't have Allan to bail you out this time."

She did have a point, so we agreed that I would make the trip on my own while Di drove up by car. This would be my most ambitious trip by far. Much of it would be out of sight of land, and I would rely entirely on the new compass. I hoped the weather stayed fair and the engine didn't quit. The reckless blood of impending middle age coursed through my veins.

I checked and rechecked my course on the charts, then checked again. I would head straight north from Toanche to the Hope Island light, then take a bearing to a point N23W (true) over the horizon. My primary target was the Red Rock light (as distinct from the Red Rock at Go-Home), a towering white navigational edifice north of the entrance to Parry Sound that can be seen for miles around. Once there, I should be able to navigate by sight to Edgar Island and the Meekison cottage.

One-third of the way along I would pass by the Westerns, a widely-dispersed group of low-lying islands spread out about 15 miles offshore. By my calculation, about 30 minutes after I passed the Westerns I should be able to pick out the Red Rock light. Accuracy was critical: if I strayed more than a couple of degrees to the west I could encounter Northeast Rock off the Westerns, while if I went off course to the east I would have to contend with a large area of unmarked shoals.

⚓ ⚓ ⚓

The day dawned warm and cloudy with a moderate northwest breeze. I didn't like the clouds one bit, for their surface reflection makes shoals difficult to see. The forecast was for continued cloudy periods and possible thunderstorms.

"Jeedge, please think again. If you must take your mistress, why don't you head across to the Pine Islands and pick up the marked channels from there? That way you'll stay away from the open water and it'll only take an extra hour."

"There's no challenge in that, love. Might just as well go by car. Tell you what. I'll wait a couple of hours, see if the weather clears. If it doesn't, then you, my dear, will have the pleasure of my company."

Then the sun came out.

⚓ ⚓ ⚓

A fresh northwest breeze whipped up small whitecaps as I emerged from the protection of Hope Island and set my course. Two miles ahead a lake freighter crossed my bow, bound for the Midland grain docks.

The chop made it impossible to navigate accurately simply by watching the compass. The Raven danced a fair jig, up and down and as much as 15 degrees in either direction. I needed to slow down, take a bearing on a distant object, and head for that. The only problem was that apart from the vanishing freighter there was no distant object: only a blank horizon. The Westerns would soon be visible, but they were off to the left, spread over a large area, useless for my purposes.

I slowed to contemplate and felt quite alone. Hope Island was now well astern; the vast horizon ahead showed nothing but the curvature of the earth. I wasn't sure how to proceed. I idly watched waves breaking over a shoal ahead, dancing high above the surrounding whitecaps. *A shoal ahead? We were supposed to be in 30 fathoms of water . . .*

Heart in mouth, I spread out the chart and tried to make sense of my position. The only shoals supposed to be within miles of Hope Island were the Watchers far to the east. I looked at the breaking waves again and realized they had moved off to the right. I had been fooled by the wake from the freighter.

Thunderclouds gathered on the northern horizon. I didn't like the idea of heading into a storm at all, but the clouds gave me an idea. A thundercloud usually stays in one place, building its force in a static way. Perhaps I could use a cloud as a navigational aid.

I nudged the Raven on course and found we were pointing directly at the nose of a large rabbit. Like Alice, I set off on my quest. After five minutes I slowed to check the bearing. The rabbit had changed shape and now had a watch in its hand, but its nose was still on course.

Soon the Westerns appeared over the horizon and I gained confidence in my unconventional technique. We passed by Northeast Rock exactly where it should be, a few hundred yards to the left. Now the rabbit's ears looped over to form an athletic support. I headed for the pointy part, where the rabbit's nose used to be.

Thirty minutes later I was sparring with a Sumo wrestler. His massive right leg was planted atop a tiny white dot. It took me a moment to realize the dot was the Red Rock light. I gave a whoop and slapped the Raven's side. She seemed to lift out of the water.

We arrived half an hour ahead of Di despite our many stops. Liz said we looked like the Great Gatsby as we entered their sheltered bay, flag streaming and pinstripe mahogany gleaming. We didn't mind that description at all, the Raven and I.

༄ ༄ ༄

For a long time after, I relished the thrill of that last trip we made together. It made me realize how much the Raven had meant to me. She had given me laughter and tears and frustration, and wonderful sweeping strokes of adventure, a foil against my humdrum daily activities. She had introduced me to outrageous characters and had taken me to improbable places. And throughout she had stayed true to her cantankerous old self.

But now the time had come to move on. I had been foolhardy enough to venture out alone across the unpredictable open waters of Georgian Bay in a leaky craft of questionable mechanical soundness, and had avoided my final comeuppance through no skill on my own part. Now I felt uncomfortable and selfish and guilty because of this.

While I was in this frame of mind, at my most vulnerable, someone told me of a new kind of boat called the Limestone 24. It was a boat, they said, built unlike any other, a boat designed specifically for the stormy waters of Georgian Bay.

I don't recall who that person was, but I do remember first seeing a Limestone. She was docked at Dutchman's Cove Marina and she swept me off my feet. Big and beamy, she had the upward-raked bow of the serious seagoing craft, a no-nonsense open cockpit, and a stepdown to a generous cuddy cabin. To bring the weight forward for improved seaworthiness, the inboard/outboard engine had been located amidships, connected to the outdrive by an ingenious jackshaft. Designed by yacht architect Mark Ellis and manufactured by Hinterhoeller Yachts of St. Catharines, Ontario, this beauty had the air of a fine sailing craft built to handle rough seas and to last a generation.

I visited the Hinterhoeller booth at the Toronto Boat Show next spring. The Limestone was surrounded by an admiring crowd. The specs said it was designed to cruise at 35 knots and that, because of its heavy construction and upthrust bow, it took the heaviest seas without shipping water or pounding. There was no question it would be ideal for our purposes. The only problem was the price, approximately double what I felt we could afford.

Still I lusted after the Limestone. That summer we visited John and Carol Macfarlane on their island near O'Donnell Point. John had just bought a Limestone and let me test drive it. One finger on the steering wheel it handled like a dream; afterwards the Raven felt ornery and unruly by comparison. Later I learned that Tony Fell, my boss at DS who also summered at Georgian Bay, had recently acquired a Limestone. That turned lust to obsession.

Poor Raven, she didn't stand a chance. Every foible irritated me, every little weakness. In response she began to give me cause. She started to leak again. Her engine would quit while at idle and refuse to restart until it had cooled down. Her bilge pump died and had to be replaced. Little things. The marina stopped carrying the regular leaded gas she required, so I was compelled to add a malodorous mixture every time I gassed up. Then one weekend, when guests arrived from Ottawa, she pulled a dreadful scene that finally sealed her fate.

⚓ ⚓ ⚓

Pam and Tony Lemoine arrived before dinner on Friday evening. They planned to spend the weekend at Toanche en route to a driving holiday up the Bruce Peninsula to Manitoulin Island and thence home. It was a beautiful evening, flat calm, and we sat on the patio watching the sun set and making plans for the next day's boating.

Di suggested we go to Ferncliffe, an island we hadn't visited in ages. Ferncliffe is in Group of Seven country, a veritable artist's paradise. It sits facing oft-painted One Tree Island (now No Tree Island, thanks to a storm in the mid-80s) and commands a panoramic view of the surrounding islands.

"Great idea. But it's quite a long trip – about five miles beyond the Pineys. Let's retire early and get a good start. We'll do our catching up tomorrow night."

Tony and I already had already made additional plans. The Toanche irrigation system had developed indigestion, and Tony, talented jack-of-all-trades, had promised to fix it. This meant we would have to return from Ferncliffe in good time.

⚓ ⚓ ⚓

Certain days etch Georgian Bay in the memory. A soft westerly rippled the water all day, and small white fluffy clouds smiled down from the bluest of blue skies. We took the northerly route to Ferncliffe, passing between Beckwith and Hope and then skirting the Watchers and the Pine Islands.

At Ferncliffe we picnicked on the warm rock and swam and snorkelled and fished. We dove off the steep ledges at the south end into the crystal water, and took too much sun. We left in good time and returned for Tony to perform his magic on the irrigation system.

I anchored the Raven in front of the cottage, intending to take her round to Albert's Cove Marina later. But by dinner's end we were mellow and it was such a beautiful evening that I decided to leave her there overnight.

We talked long into the evening. Pam is Di's cousin and they hadn't seen each other in more than a year. Occasionally I got up to check the Raven as she hung there motionless, ghostly image on the moonlit water. Curiously she was never in the same place – she drifted with the lightest air currents. But she gave no sign of impending disaster. Eventually we retired.

ॐ ॐ ॐ

"Gordon, wake up!"

"Hunh?"

Someone was shaking my shoulder. The alarm said 5:30 A.M.

"Gordon, come quick. Your boat's on the rocks!"

I shot out of bed, groped around for my running shoes, crammed them on and ran out the door, laces flying, checking I still had my pyjama pants on. Lucky.

Tony was just ahead of me, heading for our neighbours' beach. A front had passed through overnight. The wind blew straight onshore, whipping whitecaps and breakers to gleaming froth against the leaden Georgian Bay dawn. The Raven was rolling sideways, taking a beating on the rocks.

I waded round the boat, bracing against the waves. I couldn't see much but she must have already sustained damage. A line stretched out from the bow into the surf. I followed it out and retrieved the anchor, hopelessly fouled. Idiot. The Raven had drifted around in the calm of the previous evening and spread the line randomly over the bottom, then, when the wind came up, she had resolutely tightened the noose and dragged the anchor nose first to the shore. Would I never learn?

I suddenly realized how cold the water was and wished I had more than pyjama pants on. But we couldn't lose any time if we wished to save the Raven. We desperately needed to push her out into deeper water. A large comber blindsided me and nearly knocked me over. I lurched back to the boat and worked my way round to join Tony on the lee side. Together we put our backs to the hull and heaved. A cord rose in Tony's neck. The Raven wouldn't budge.

Di and Pam came running down to help. Quite a picture, the four of us scantily clad, digging our heels in and fighting the waves, trying to keep our footing. We gave a concerted thrust just as a spuming wall of water lifted the boat half out of the water and sent us sprawling. I fell hard and skinned my elbow as the Raven crunched down inches from Di's foot.

I scrambled up and waved the others off. A red stain spread on my torn pyjama sleeve. The howling wind, the crashing waves and a cold aching dullness around my groin provided appropriate dramatic background.

"Back off, everybody, take a breather, not worth broken bones," I shouted into the wind.

The boat lifted and thumped down several times as we stood there. It was more than I could stand.

"Hell, there's no other way, we have to try again. Just have to time it right with the next big wave, push like crazy when she lifts."

Tony and I braced our backs against the hull as a roller frothed towards us. Di and Pam hesitated, then joined in the fray.

"Hold her now . . . hold her . . . ready . . . **heave!**"

The Raven lifted neatly off the rocks and slid back into the waves. I scrambled over the side and fired up the motor then gunned straight out, narrowly missing a boulder just off our neighbours' dock. A hundred yards out I started to turn and waved at the three pyjama-clad figures on the shore. Then the engine sputtered and water gushed in.

There was no time, no question of stuffing rags into the breach: I had no idea where she was holed, nor any inclination to find out. She was listing hard to port and I prepared to abandon ship. The Raven's time had come. *This is it, old girl, best way to go, over with no recriminations. Insurance should provide a nice down payment on the Limestone . . .*

A low moan came from beneath the deck – the wind playing tricks. I gave the cockpit a last lingering look. There in its waterproof case lay the chart with the course from Hope Island to Red Rock Light still marked in red; and there above it the Newfoundland fisherman's box compass, its date of installation, July 1986, inscribed on the hand crafted mahogany frame. Suddenly these items seemed so personal, the memories so real.

My life with the Raven kaleidoscoped before me: John Frise grinning with arms spread wide, newspaper in hand . . . the Raven in the Gores Landing boat shed covered in swallow droppings . . . purring, snarling, throbbing against my fingertips at Bensfort Bridge . . . Tramp in mid-flight . . . the lockkeeper with the weepy eye . . . the Oriental fishermen watching our undignified retreat . . . John Frise singing, wind in silver hair . . . the electric storm on Lake Simcoe . . . Frise proffering Kleenex to his water cannon victims . . . Peter and Gay Regan introducing us to Thompson's Point . . . Peter rhapsodizing over the Raven . . . Jim Fletcher and Paul Spafford loading the Raven to the gunwales at the Penetang dock . . . the Green family assembled on duty watch at the Thompson's

Point gazebo . . . Fletcher and Spafford, eyes downcast, the Raven under
tow . . . the soles of Terence's feet . . . Walley racing in the other Raven . . .
the Keystone Cops on Lake Champlain . . . empty Chablis on the rocks
with the Taylors . . . Di concealing her bikini on the Essex ferry . . . Art
and son barring the way over the Adirondacks . . . Doris Gibson surrounded by floating garbage bags . . . Bill van Rijn rubbing his hands, the
Raven growling . . . Allan Crosbie lost in the *Economist* . . . John Frise in
hospital . . . John Frise singing . . . John Frise . . .

A second moan, lower yet and softer, brought me back with a jolt. I
had to save her, no time to lose. If I could just keep the engine running,
maybe I could beach her in the sand beside our neighbours' dock and
lash her to the cribbing to ride out the storm. The dock, one of the few
on the entire shore, was built of massive cribs and was protected by a
groyne. If anything could save the Raven, that would.

The engine kept sputtering long enough to bring her in. Water was
sloshing all about the cabin. I shouted to Tony to fetch additional lines
as I beached the Raven in the sand against the dock. The engine quit as
we grounded.

The waves still inflicted a fearful pounding, but we placed an old tire
between dock and boat and lashed the Raven from several points to the
cribbing. That way she rode out the storm.

ッ ッ ッ

"Hubert, it's Gordon. My boat went up on the rocks and now she's
beached on my neighbours' property, leaking badly. How can I get her
back to you so you can put her in the slings and lift her out?"

"Pump her out, then keep her pumped while you tow her over."

"Bilge pump'll never keep up. Like peeing against Niagara Falls."

"Then borrow my gas-powered fire pump. But wait till the weather
settles a bit."

After lunch we drove to the marina to pick up the pump while the
girls settled down for a chat. They were still at it when Tony and I got
back and went to work. Helpful bits of advice floated down from Pam
in the hammock and Di in the chaise longue. They had to shout to be
heard over the noise of the pump.

"Tony, you'll get gas all over your pants and you'll never get rid of the
smell."

"Jeedge, turn that infernal machine off! The neighbours!"

Soon the Raven floated free in the calmer water and we set off, Tony
manning the pump and I towing the Raven in the small outboard. The

huge rooster tail thrown by the pump scribed artistic patterns, occasionally dousing me. Di and Pam taunted us about tilting at windmills.

Pam turned to Di. "Tony's never been so happy, Di. I bet you arranged this whole thing just to keep him busy!"

When we reached the marina Hubert swung the Raven high in the slings and water poured from a gaping hole in her bow. Her prop was a mangled mess, her rudder askew. It was almost the end.

                              ⚓ ⚓ ⚓

John Fuller took the news with equanimity.

"All these years since the last accident, Gordon. Obviously you took my bathtub advice to heart. Any good wooden boat specialists near you?"

"Not sure, except of course in Penetang."

"Never mind, the adjuster will look into it. That's his job."

Charles Blondin of Lafontaine was an excellent boat builder who had a fine reputation for completely restoring wooden boats. The adjuster made the financial arrangements directly with Blondin. The only thing I had to do was co-sign the insurance company's cheque when the repairs were finished.

                              ⚓ ⚓ ⚓

The last time I saw the Raven she sat on her rusty trailer in front of Blondin's shop. She really did look spiffy, sparkling with replacement ribs and planks, a completely fresh finish and a shiny new brass propeller. I felt a pang.

The antique boat broker from Muskoka rolled up in his pickup. He looked the Raven over, walked around her appreciatively, whistled as he swept his hand along her sides. Then he nodded briefly, hooked her up and drove off. As they climbed Lafontaine Hill, the Raven's transom wiggled saucily on the uneven surface.

I didn't wave. Just stood there and watched her disappear. Then took a deep breath and headed back to the marina and the new Limestone.

ABOUT THE AUTHOR

Gordon Green came to Canada from England in
1956 and attended University of British Columbia
and the Harvard Business School. He spent most
of his career negotiating the treacherous canyons
of Bay Street and Wall Street, travelling across
Canada advising and arranging financings for
Canadian corporations and governments. Endowed
with a streak of irreverence that sometimes gets
him into trouble, Green has a passion for the Arts
and for all things outdoors. He now makes his
home in Sidney, British Columbia, where he lives
on the ocean with his wife Diana and their two
dogs. He currently serves as President of Pacific
Opera Victoria and has several corporate
directorships as well. **The Raven and I** is his first
book.

L. MICHIGAN

L. HURON

L. ONTARIO

L. ERIE

AREAS OF
DETAIL

GEORGIAN

BAY

LAKE

HURON

45°

Parry Sound

Go-Home Bay

Honey Harbour

Christian I.

Port Severn

Toanche

Penetanguishene

L. Couchiching

Orillia

Owen
Sound

L.
SIMCOE

Barrie

44°

Toronto

0   50   Miles

0   50   Kilometers

81°   80°

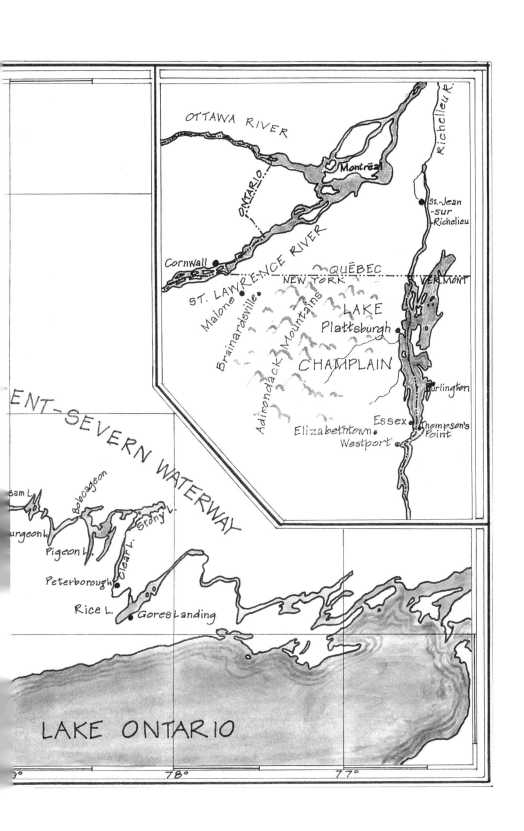